Bewitching
Bead & Wire Jewelry

Bewitching
Bead & Wire Jewelry

Easy Techniques for 40 Irresistible Projects

Designs by 27 Leading Artists

Suzanne J.E. Tourtillott

LARK JEWELRY
& BEADING

**EDITOR &
PHOTOGRAPHER**
Suzanne J.E. Tourtillott

**ART DIRECTOR &
COVER DESIGNER**
Mary McGahren

ILLUSTRATOR
Melissa Grakowsky Shippee

LARK CRAFTS
An Imprint of Sterling Publishing
387 Park Avenue South
New York, NY 10016

ISBN 978-1-4547-0756-1

Library of Congress Cataloging-in-Publication Data

Tourtillott, Suzanne J. E.
  Bewitching bead & wire jewelry : easy techniques for 40 irresistible projects / Suzanne Tourtillott. -- First edition.
    pages cm
  ISBN 978-1-4547-0756-1 (pbk.)
  1. Beadwork. 2. Jewelry making. I. Title.
  TT860.T778 2013
  745.594'2--dc23
                          2012033478

Distributed in Canada by Sterling Publishing
c/o Canadian Manda Group, 165 Dufferin Street
Toronto, Ontario, Canada M6K 3H6
Distributed in the United Kingdom by GMC Distribution Services
Castle Place, 166 High Street, Lewes, East Sussex, England BN7 1XU
Distributed in Australia by Capricorn Link (Australia) Pty. Ltd.
P.O. Box 704, Windsor, NSW 2756, Australia

For information about custom editions, special sales, and premium and corporate purchases, please contact Sterling Special Sales at 800-805-5489 or specialsales@sterlingpublishing.com.

Email academic@larkbooks.com for information about desk and examination copies.
The complete policy can be found at larkcrafts.com.

Manufactured in China

2 4 6 8 10 9 7 5 3 1

larkcrafts.com

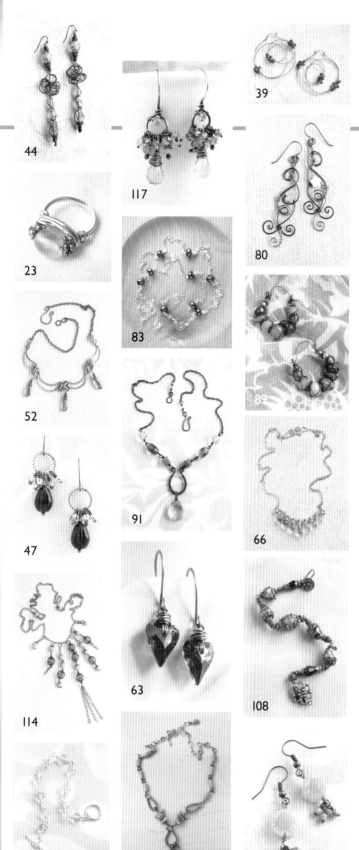

Contents

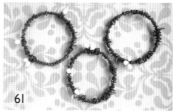

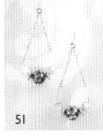

What You'll Need

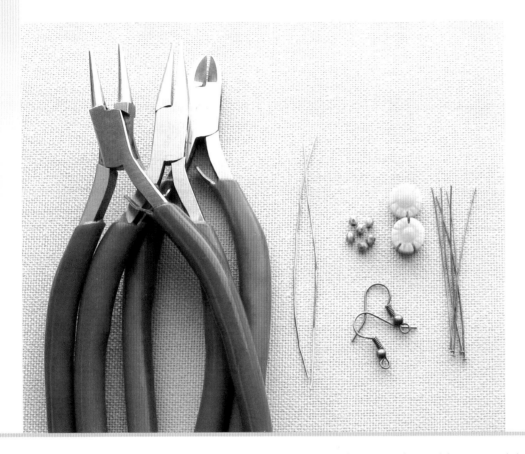

With these basic materials and easy-to-learn techniques, you'll have everything you need to make the projects in this book. From smooth to twisty, gleaming to matte, beads and wire are easily found, so you can start creating these great designs right away.

BEADS...AND MORE BEADS

A quick look at intriguing beads, similar to those used for the projects in this book, shows that a bead can be darn well anything with a smallish hole in it somewhere. But let's look at the possibilities in greater detail.

Gemstones might gleam softly or flash brilliantly, depending on the type of stone, its cut, and its finish. Classic semiprecious stones such as turquoise, citrine, and garnet are often shaped into rounds or tubes, then drilled and tumbled smooth. But don't limit yourself to the known! Branch out and discover the family of amethysts (colors range from pale pink to deep, "royal" purple) as well as stones like sodalite, jasper, and quartz. Beads are cut into faceted rounds, smooth teardrops, chunky squares, and more.

Glass beads are a world of their own. The wildly popular *cut-crystal* and *cut-glass* faceted beads are cut into shapes with exotic-sounding names like rondelle, briolette, and bicone. One subtype has a "fire-polished" finish for a subtle flash of iridescence. Seemingly, the number of color combinations is vast, which only makes for some challenging yet fun shopping. Most jewelry dimensions are given in the metric system; like wire sizing, some glass beads have their own "size language" (standardized dimensions and hole sizes). Another glass style is the handmade *lamp worked* bead. These are their own intricate, swirly art form and are often sold individually by their makers.

Solid *metal* beads are often small because they're heavy. Larger ones are lighter if they use an openwork design. Filigree, bumps, and texture wanted? Go to Bali, where all manner of barrel, pipe, square, and tube beads are made. The intricate textures of *bali silver* beads are often enhanced by an oxidation (darkening of metal) process.

Wooden beads, bone beads, pearls, and other bead wonderments are also waiting to be discovered. Ceramic, resin, and plastic beads can add unexpected new textures to a jewelry piece. Be not afraid, explorer; sally forth and find more beads!

WIRE OPTIONS

Once upon a time, bead and wire jewelry was made only with precious-metal wire—basically, gold or silver. Today, you have choices—myriad choices. Each wire type has unique working qualities. Here's an introduction to some common types of wire, so you can navigate the dozens of options in workability, color, size, and finish.

TYPES OF WIRE

Bright, versatile, affordable *silver wire*: what's not to love? Using techniques that you'll learn a little later on, you'll find that silver is the ultimate chameleon in the wire-jewelry world. Besides silver's superior shapeability, all kinds of surface-finishing methods are possible with it. (More about that in Techniques, page 14.) Silver is sold according to its degree of malleability (*hard*, *half-hard*, *soft*, and *dead soft*), profile (round, square, and half-round are the basic ones), and purity (*sterling* suits most projects just fine). If a wire's hardness isn't mentioned in the project instructions, use half-hard wire. It will get a little stiffer, or *work-hardened*, through the bending and shaping. If you're concerned about an allergic reaction to

an alloy metal, consider the purer form called *argentium silver*.

As for surface qualities, sterling's bright finish tarnishes, but silver-free *German style* wire does not. And silver's smooth-shiny surface can easily pick up kinks and tool nicks. You might want to practice a design first with a lower-cost wire. More about how to finish silver will be covered in Techniques, on page 17.

Lustrous, butter-soft, and totally classic *gold-filled wire*—actually, brass wire bonded with a thin layer of gold—is more expensive than silver. (*Plated* gold will flake off when it's bent, so stay away from it.) Gold is alloyed with other metals and the purity of the resulting blend is expressed in karats, from

---

DESIGNER'S TIP: Choose the wire that best fits the bead's hole, without any drag or snag.

10-karat to 24-karat. Varying the alloy metal and proportions results in even more hardness grades than those for silver, and alloyed gold doesn't tarnish. You can buy either spools or custom-cut, coiled lengths of silver or gold wire.

For affordable options and deep metallic coloration, non-tarnish *brass* and *copper* are good wire choices. Want bright color with your soft and malleable copper? *Craft wire* has a pigmented enamel coating that ensures a veritable rainbow of hue choices, in both glossy metallic and satin-matte finishes. This dead-soft wire has some drawbacks. While not as strong as some other wire types, craft wire keeps its shape well enough, though your hardness and surface-finishing choices may be fewer. Be sure to determine whether the product is hypoallergenic or not before you buy it.

Other wire types, like memory wire and piano wire, weren't used for any of our projects, but that doesn't mean you couldn't explore them at some point in your wire-wrapping adventures. (A caution about anodized niobium wire:

the bright colors are nice but not long lasting. Like artistic wire, niobium is inexpensive and therefore great for practicing technique.)

WIRE SIZING

Gauge is the number that expresses the thickness of a wire. You'll want to know a bit about the gauge numbering system to make informed purchases. The one quirky fact about gauge numbers is the larger the number, the thinner, or finer, that wire actually is. For example, 22-gauge wire is much thinner than 12-gauge. Manufacturers in the United States use the AWG/B&S system; in the United Kingdom, it's SWG. (*Note:* U.S. and U.K. gauge numbers aren't interchangeable, but within either system you'll find that any single gauge of wire—whether gold, artistic, or brass—will always be of standard thickness.) Rather perversely, bead hole and jump ring diameters are measured only in millimeters—not gauge size. To make sure a bead you are thinking of buying online will fit a wire (or vice versa), find gauge-millimeter equivalents in the Wire Gauge Chart on page 123.

WIRE HARDNESS AND SHAPE

A word about workability: a wire's position on the hardness scale gives an indication of how stiff it is. Softer wire is of course easier to work with, but also shows tool marks more readily. Harder wire is less forgiving of change in angle

and direction, but obviously it stays put better. As you work one of the softer wires, it can become work-hardened. Even bending or hammering wire makes it stiffer. If you're just starting out, consider using a softer and less expensive wire to practice your swoops and bends and wraps before moving on to the pricier stuff.

Thought wire was only round? Think again! A wire's *profile* (the shape if it is cut crosswise) can also be half-round or square. Craft wire is also made in "fancy round" and "fancy square" profiles.

FINDINGS

What's that word for the little thingies that help turn wire and beads into a finished jewelry piece? Glad you asked: it's *findings*. Here's a quick overview of the connectors that bring it all together.

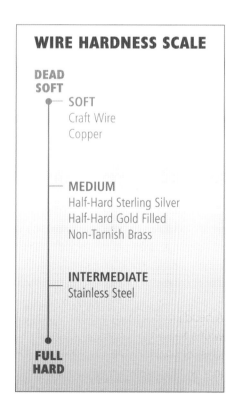

WIRE HARDNESS SCALE

DEAD SOFT

— **SOFT**
Craft Wire
Copper

— **MEDIUM**
Half-Hard Sterling Silver
Half-Hard Gold Filled
Non-Tarnish Brass

— **INTERMEDIATE**
Stainless Steel

FULL HARD

A jump ring is a small, plain circle made from round wire. You use it to join two elements—say, a link in a chain to a loop in a wire. The *open jump ring* has been helpfully sawed through on one side, so you can open and close it. Match or contrast the metal, gauge, and sizes of your jump rings to the rest of the wire in your piece, as well as to its overall scale. *Closed jump rings* have been soldered shut. You can still use them to join elements, usually with wire loops.

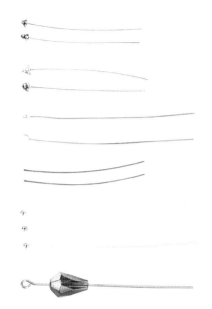

Ear wires are shaped earring wires with connector loops that you open like jump rings. Commercial ones offer a limited choice of metal, finish, and in some cases gauge. One-of-a-kind, handmade wires add a striking look and are easy to master.

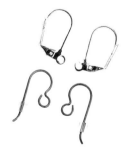

A *head pin* is a straight piece of wire with a flat or fancy balled end, made of silver or gold or some other metal and in a range of wire gauges and lengths.

Clasps connect the ends of a necklace or a bracelet. They, too, come in many different finishes and metal types. The trigger-style clasp is most familiar, but lobster clasps are quite popular, too. You'll find a wide variety of commercially made toggle clasps, for a streamlined look and quick connection. Many

of the projects in this book have unique, handmade clasps and ear wires whose designs make unique complements to the rest of the wirework.

While not quite a finding in the strictest sense of the word, *commercial chain* is a popular element in bead and wire designs. A simpler design won't distract from your beautiful work but will instead understatedly pair with it. Cut through a link to make it into the desired length.

DESIGNER'S TIP: For perfectly matched chain lengths, fold one length in half. Grasp the two free ends, letting the chain hang in midair. Cut through the bottommost link.

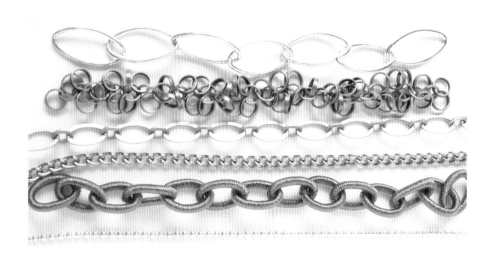

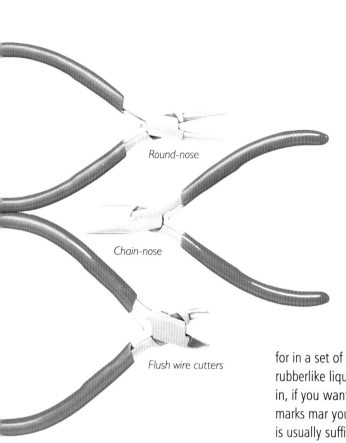

Round-nose

Chain-nose

Flush wire cutters

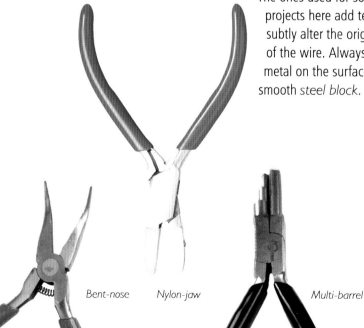

Steel block

TOOLS

A small tool kit of the most common jewelry-making tools will be needed for the projects in this book. After the basic ones are explored, some optional pieces are introduced.

The first thing you always do with wire is cut it, so sharpness is all. The less-expensive implements are made with softer cutting edges, so if cost is an issue, a mid-priced choice may be your best compromise. You can always upgrade later. Better-quality *flush wire cutters* make a clean cut through wire and leave no burr. And fewer burrs will mean less filing for you.

For the frequent turning and repositioning of the pliers' jaws, you'll want good control. Grip comfort, as well as the degree and tightness of the spring mechanism, are the top qualities to look

for in a set of pliers. (There's even a rubberlike liquid you can coat the jaws in, if you want to be quite certain no marks mar your wire. But a light hand is usually sufficient.)

The jaws of *round-nose* pliers are conical. To make a full curl or loop or circle in a wire, use these. *Flat-nose* pliers have flat jaws to use for nicely angled turns. *Chain-nose* pliers also have round jaws, but with flat inner surfaces for gripping and bending wire.

Specialty pliers do more specific jobs, but most can be considered optional—especially if you're just starting to make bead and wire jewelry. *Bent chain-nose* pliers are nearly tweezerlike in their ability to precisely pinch and grasp and tuck wire into tight spots. The jaws of *multi-barrel* pliers have mandrel-like stepped sections that let you make the same size loop or curl every time. Use *nylon-jaw* pliers to straighten kinked wire.

Unlike a carpenter's hammer, the *jeweler's hammer* has a super-smooth head, so it won't scratch or nick metal. Each style of head has a different purpose. The ones used for some of the projects here add texture and subtly alter the original shape of the wire. Always hammer metal on the surface of a very smooth *steel block*.

Bent-nose   *Nylon-jaw*   *Multi-barrel*

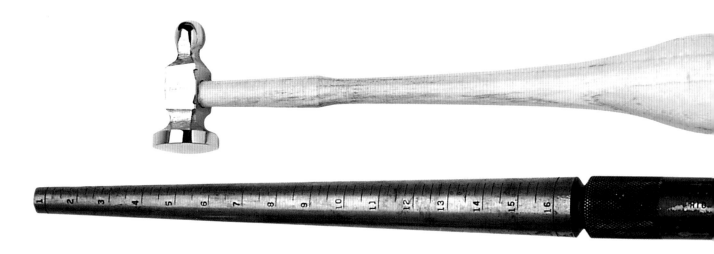

A *mandrel* can be any smooth, curved object that you shape your wire around. (Actually, one jaw of a pair of round-nose pliers works well as a small mandrel.) The larger loops and swirls can usually be formed over the mandrel with just your fingers rather than a tool. You can buy a set of jeweler's mandrels, but in many cases a marker or other household item of similar diameter can work just as well. Measure the mandrel using a sizing gauge (see tool at bottom right) if you need a specific diameter.

TOOL KIT AT A GLANCE

Round-nose pliers

Chain-nose pliers

2 pairs of flat-nosed pliers

Flush wire cutters

Jeweler's hammer

Steel block

Mandrel

Needle files

NICE TO HAVE

Jewelry *needle files* are quite small and rather delicate looking. You can usually buy a nice set that includes a range of profiles and cuts, from coarse to fine. Even though using flush wire cutters reduces unwanted *burrs*, you'll also want to file the ends of cut wire for a snag-free finish. See page 15 for how to deal with burrs.

The *sizing gauge* is a handy tool that measures inner diameters (of bead holes, jump rings, and mandrels) and also the diameter of wire. (Don't let it confuse you; a gauge can be a tool as well as a wire's size number!) Match a measured wire diameter to the gauge number in the Wire Gauge Chart on page 123.

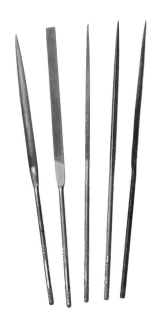

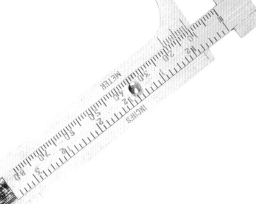

Techniques

Many of the projects in this book wrangle jewelry wire in ways that no one's ever thought of before. But even the most unusual designs also rely on tried-and-true wireworking methods. Learning these basic techniques helps you practice before you navigate the project instructions.

WIRE

Keeping stored wire smooth and ready for action can be a challenge. Store lengths of wire flat and keep unruly wire spools in plastic bags. Use a slip of anti-tarnish paper in your boxes and bags to reduce the effects of oxidation on precious metals.

When you're ready to work with a shorter piece of wire, first straighten it. Grasp one end of the piece in a pair of pliers and pull the last little bit of curve out of it by running it through a cloth held between your fingers (so you don't get a friction burn). You might use a jeweler's *rouge cloth*: start with the red, compound-loaded side, and make a second pass with the yellow buffing side. Another option is to pull wire straight through a pair of nylon-coated flat-nose pliers—it works really well on longer pieces.

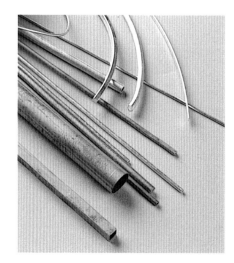

CURLS, LOOPS, SPIRALS, AND WRAPS

Bead and wire jewelry connections are made from ingenious curves and turns. Once you know the fundamental methods for handling wire with pliers, you'll see that designs are often unique combinations and embellishments of basic techniques.

Throughout this book, the project instructions call for making wire cuts with flush wire cutters. These cutters leave much less of a ragged edge at the cut. Take extra precaution by gently filing each of your cuts before you start the wirework. A jewelry file's finely ground surface ensures that you'll have no snags or tears from sharp wire ends.

A simple wire loop is the first turn in a *spiral*. You make the loop by grasping one end of a piece of wire between the jaws of a pair of round-nose pliers. Hold the long tail in your other hand, make a turn of the pliers, and you've done your first bit of wirework (figure 1).

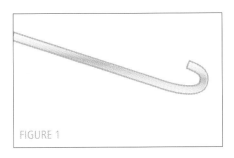

FIGURE 1

Shift the pliers down the tail from the simple loop and turn them again a time or two; a spiral appears (figure 2).

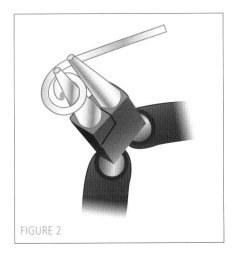

FIGURE 2

For a really substantial spiral, change to flat-nose pliers and use your fingers to guide the wire into the outer turns (figure 3).

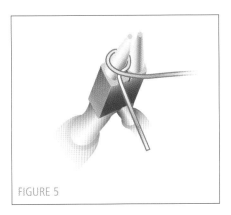

FIGURE 3

CONNECTIONS

A popular way to make a join with wire is to create a *wrapped loop*. Start with a straight section of wire. An inch (2.5 cm) or so away from one end of it, use a pair of round-nose pliers to make a 90° bend in it (figure 4).

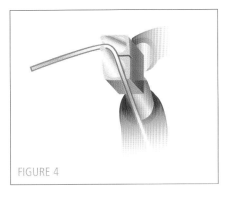

FIGURE 4

Shift the pliers away from the bend and make a full curl, or *loop*, in the shorter wire, using your other hand to bring the curl's tail across the straight wire (figure 5). This is the wrapping wire.

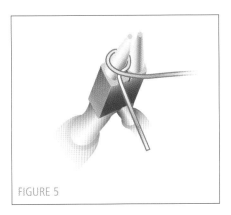

FIGURE 5

Using the pliers to hold the loop, close up the loop's open base by bringing the wrapping wire around the straight wire two or three times (figure 6).

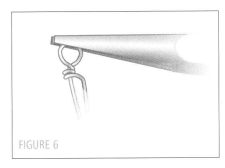

FIGURE 6

Snip the wrapping wire closely with good, sharp flush wire cutters (figure 7).

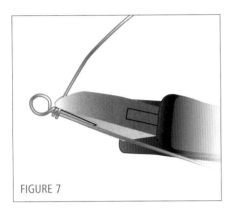

FIGURE 7

You might slip a bead onto the straight wire and add another wrapped loop at the other end of the wire. Then you'd have a *bead loop link* (it can act like a link in a chain). Make a *dangle* by capturing a bead with a wrapped loop at the open end of a head pin (figure 8).

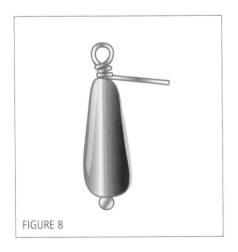

FIGURE 8

Sometimes space is so tight that two pairs of chain-nose pliers can control the wire better than your fingers can (figure 9).

SAME SIZE LOOPS (EVERY TIME!)

With a permanent marker, draw a line on one jaw of a pair of round-nose pliers. If you place your wire there every time you make a loop, they'll all be the same size.

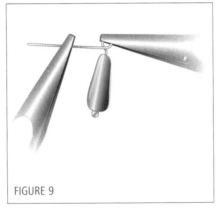

FIGURE 9

Wire wrapping can be careful and neat, or exuberant and a little bit messy. A *wire cap loop* (sometimes called a "tornado wrap") may look unplanned, but it's a neat and attractive way to hide a bead hole. It's particularly effective for top-drilled teardrop-shaped beads. First, pass the wire through the hole, and cross the wires at the top of the bead.

Make two turns of a wrap with one of the crossed tails, then cut it closely (figure 10). Holding the wire with the round-nose pliers close to the last wrap, make a full loop in the wire. Hold the loop in a pair of flat-nose pliers and start wrapping down. Cover those first wraps, and continue wrapping the wire down over the top of the bead. Don't try to make it too neat.

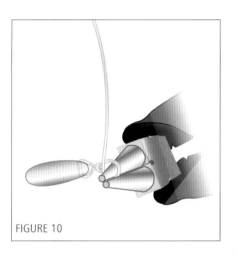

FIGURE 10

When you've wrapped far enough down to cover the bead's hole, wrap the wire back up to just under the loop. Trim it closely with wire cutters (figure 11) and press the cut end in well with the tips of a pair of chain-nose pliers.

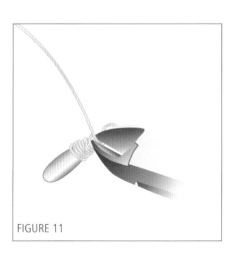

FIGURE 11

Jump rings should be opened in a certain way, usually with the aid of flat-nose pliers. Holding the ring so that the opening is at 12 o'clock, grasp the ring on one side with the pliers. Grasp the other side with a second pair of flat-nose pliers and torque the ends away from each other (figure 12). Never pull the ends apart laterally—the metal might crack.

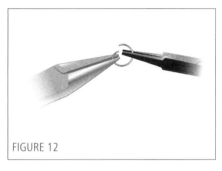

FIGURE 12

FINISHING

The alteration of the natural color of a metal surface results in a *patina*. With jewelry, this is usually accomplished by covering the metal with some sort of chemical solution that interacts with the metal and creates color or a darkening called *oxidation*. Commercial products like liver of sulfur for silver, and oxidizers for brass, bronze, and copper, are all commercially available. Your metal must be first cleaned of the oils from your hands, and other precautions observed, so be sure to follow the manufacturer's instructions.

After all is said and done, there's polishing. All metal looks better if it's polished. You can hand-buff the dark patina from just the raised surfaces of silver with very fine steel wool, or get a high polish by means of an electric tumbler. Its container gently abrades the entire jewelry piece with *shot* (like tiny BBs) in a solution of soapy water. The manufacturer will provide guidelines for what can and what should not be tumbled. Don't tumble-polish a project in this book unless the instructions say so.

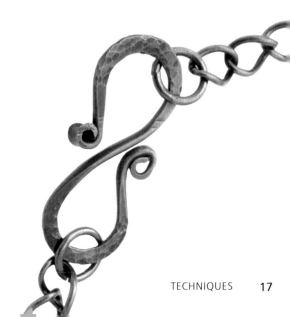

Designed by **COCO KULKARNI**

Red Bone Necklace

Gleaming silver against deep-red bone equals superior style in this statement piece!

MATERIALS

2 red bone round beads, 25 mm

1 red bone bugle bead, 23 mm

3 pieces of silver-plated 18-gauge non-tarnish wire, 18 inches (45.7 cm) long

3 inches (7.6 cm) of silver-plated 16-gauge non-tarnish wire

2 pieces of 3-mm silver-plated link chain, each 6 inches (15.2 cm) long

2 jump rings, 18 gauge, 6 mm

2 jump rings, 18 gauge, 8 mm

TOOLS

Needle-nose pliers

Round-nose pliers

Bent-nose pliers

2 pairs of flat-nose pliers

Flush wire cutters

Needle file

Ballpoint pen, for a mandrel

Rawhide mallet and steel block

DIMENSIONS

Length, 18 inches (45.7 cm)

INSTRUCTIONS

1 To form a loop, first use needle-nose pliers to bend one piece of the 18-gauge wire at a 90° angle, 1½ inches (3.8 cm) from one end.

2 Make the loop with round-nose pliers, then use the bent-nose pliers to wrap the short wire around the loop two or three times. Cut any excess wire. Smooth any cut edges with a needle file. Press the wire end flat with the bent-nose pliers.

3 Slide a round bead onto the long wire and down to the loop. Bend the straight wire at a 90° angle on top of the bead and form a wrapped loop there, leaving some additional space for spirals underneath the loop. Holding the loop firmly in your flat-nose pliers, form a four-turn spiral under this second loop that you just made (figure 1).

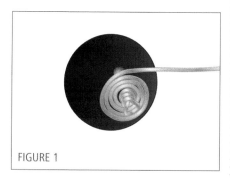

FIGURE 1

4 Shape the wire around to the bead's other hole and form four spirals there too (figure 2). Cut the excess wire at an angle and smooth the cut end with the file. Tuck the end into the spiral with the bent-nose pliers.

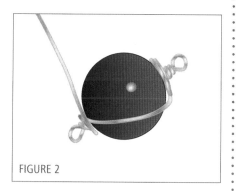

FIGURE 2

5 With a new piece of 18-gauge wire, form a new loop. Insert the short end of the loop wire into one of the wrapped bead's loops (figure 3). Complete the wrapping of the loop. This makes a strong link.

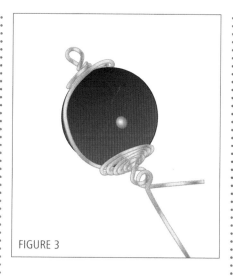

FIGURE 3

6 Slide in the long tube bead, then make a second wrapped loop at the other end. Form four spirals, leaving the wire uncut. Shape it across the bead to the wrapped loop at the other end. Cut the excess wire at an angle, smooth it, and tuck in the end.

7 Repeat steps 5 and 6 with the last piece of 18-gauge wire and the second round bead.

8 Smooth both ends of the 16-gauge wire with the needle file. Using the round-nose pliers, make a small loop at one end of the wire. Make another loop at the other end, in the opposite direction of the first loop.

9 Hold the mandrel tightly right next to one of these loops. Form the wire over the mandrel, toward the other end, to form a large loop. Repeat the shaping process at the other end of the wire (figure 4).

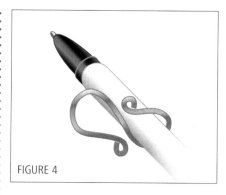

FIGURE 4

10 Now you have an S-shaped clasp, though it may be slightly askew. Place it on the steel block and gently flatten it with the mallet.

11 Use the 6-mm jump rings to attach a section of silver chain at each open loop end of the three joined beads. Attach the other two jump rings to the other end of the chains.

12 Slide an 8-mm jump ring onto each end of the S-hook clasp and attach these to the 6-mm jump rings.

Silver & Moonstone Drops

Glowing moonstone against darkened wire… it's easy to see where the inspiration came from.

Designed by KAMMY PIETRASZEK

MATERIALS

2 gray moonstone briolettes, 8 x 8 mm

4 pink Peruvian opal rondelles, 4 mm

2 pieces of sterling silver wire, 26 gauge, each 6½ inches (16.5 cm) long

4 pieces of sterling silver wire, 26 gauge, each 3½ inches (8.9 cm) long

2 pieces of sterling silver wire, 21 gauge, each 2 inches (5.1 cm) long

TOOLS

Chain-nose pliers

Round-nose pliers

Flush wire cutters

Permanent marker

Wooden dowels, ¼ inch (6 mm) and 5/16 inch (8 mm) in diameter

Ball-peen hammer and steel block

Jeweler's file

Liver of sulfur

Steel wool, grade 0000

Tweezers

Pretreated polishing pad

DIMENSIONS

Length, 1⅞ inches (4.8 cm)

INSTRUCTIONS

MOONSTONE LINK

1 String a moonstone briolette to the midpoint of one of the 6½-inch (16.5 cm) wires.

2 Fold both ends of the wire over the top of the briolette so they cross each other. Using the chain-nose pliers, bend the wires so that they are vertically aligned (figure 1).

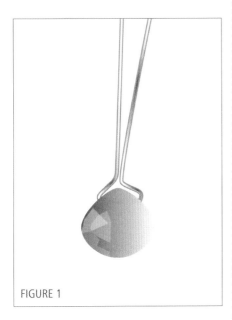

FIGURE 1

3 Grasping the pair of wires at the same time with the round-nose pliers, create a simple loop (figure 2). Now wrap the

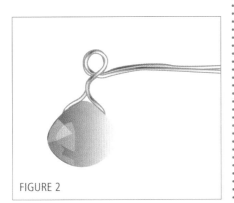

FIGURE 2

pair of wires around the base of the simple loop two or three times. With each turn, bring the wire as close as possible to the top of the briolette into a pleasing wire cap. Clip off the ends of the wire with the flush wire cutters and tuck them in at the back of the cap.

4 Repeat steps 1–3 for the other briolette.

OPAL SPIRAL LINK

5 Turn a half-loop 1⅝ inches (4 cm) from one end of a 3½-inch (8.9 cm) piece of wire. Catch one of the moonstone links in the half-loop. Close the loop by making two or three close wraps. Leave the tail for now.

6 Add an opal bead to the wire and close it with another two or three close wraps, as shown in figure 3. Use the tail to make two or three spiraling turns at the top of the bead, as shown in figure 4. Clip the ends of the wires at the back of the bead. Do the same for the other tail (from step 5).

FIGURE 3

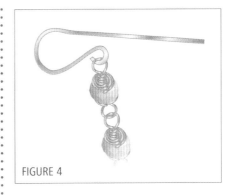

FIGURE 4

7 Attach a second opal bead link to the one you made in steps 5 and 6.

8 Repeat steps 5–7 to make a second bead dangle.

EAR WIRES

9 Use the permanent marker to mark one jaw of the round-nose pliers 2 mm from the tip. Use this mark to create a simple loop at one end of each of the 21-gauge wires. These will be the loops that hold the dangles.

10 Make a mark ⅜ inch (1 cm) down from the loop end of the wire you turned in step 9. Repeat for the other wire.

11 Lay the wires, side by side, over the ¼-inch (6 mm) dowel. The marks should be centered at the topmost curve of the dowel. Curve both wires over the dowel at the same time (figure 5).

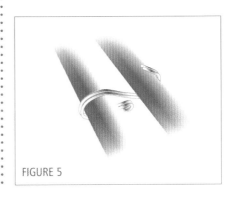

FIGURE 5

Silver & Moonstone Drops

I2 Holding the pair of ear wires together by their loops as they remain curved over the ¼-inch (6 mm) dowel, lay the ⁵⁄₁₆-inch (8 mm) dowel on top of the ear wires' midsection. Create the ear wires' large "earlobe curves" by forming them up from under the dowel.

I3 Use the ball-peen hammer and the bench block to flatten the front-facing parts of the ear wires (including the small loops). Use the chain-nose pliers to squeeze the dangle loops shut (they will open slightly from the hammering). Reshape the wires as necessary, to make sure they match.

I4 Hold the non-loop ends of the ear wires against the ⁵⁄₁₆-inch (8 mm) dowel. Use the ¼-inch (6 mm) dowel to curve the wire ends slightly. Keeping the ear wires on the dowel, clip the ends to the desired length. Remove the ear wires from the dowel and file their ends. Lightly hammer these last curves.

I5 Use the chain-nose pliers to open the small loops on the ear wires, as you would open a jump ring. Add the bead links to the opened loops, and then close them.

FINAL FINISH

I6 Oxidize the metal in a solution of liver of sulfur and scalding-hot water. Let the solution work until the silver parts have turned black.

I7 Remove the earrings from the solution, rinse them in cool tap water, then let them dry on a paper towel. Carefully polish the silver with steel wool so that the raised surfaces become lighter. Use tweezers to pick out any stray pieces of steel wool that may have become caught in the earrings.

I8 Use the polishing pad to give the sterling silver a final polish.

Designed by **MARIE CASTIGLIA**

Blue Glass Ring

Attain effortless, beachy style with a single seaglass tube bead and a few swoops of gold wire.

MATERIALS

4 gold-colored daisy spacer beads, 8 mm

1 wavy blue frosted-glass bead, 10 mm

10 inches (25.4 cm) of half-round, 18-gauge gold-filled wire*

* This is enough wire for any ring size.

TOOLS

Chain-nose pliers

Ring mandrel

Chasing hammer

Flush wire cutters

Flat needle file

DIMENSIONS

Ring size: 9½ (2½ inches, or 6.4 cm in diameter)

INSTRUCTIONS

1 String two of the spacer beads, the blue bead, and the other two spacer beads onto the center of the gold wire.

2 Place the flat side of the half-round wire on the mandrel at the desired ring size, keeping the group of beads together and facing you.

3 Make the ring band by bringing the wire's ends around the mandrel twice, crossing them as shown in figure 1.

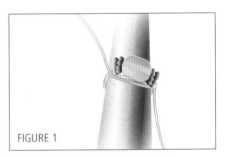

FIGURE 1

Resist the urge to do much adjusting, though, so that the band keeps its smooth, round shape.

4 Hammer all around the band, gently, to help maintain the circular shape.

5 Bring the right tail clockwise around the base of the beads twice. Wrap the left tail counterclockwise twice around the base of the beads.

6 With the ring still on the mandrel, wrap two more times—first right, then left—where the beads meet the band.

7 Cut the excess wire from the tails with the flush wire cutters.

8 The wire ends are very sharp. File them gently with the flat needle file until they feel smooth.

9 Use the chain-nose pliers to flatten the ends against the band.

Designed by KENDRA TORNHEIM

Emerald crystals flash in a coppery cuff of flowing wirework.

Copper
Leaf
Bracelet

MATERIALS

3 antiqued copper oak leaf elements, each 1 inch (2.5 cm) long

6 emerald green bicone crystals, 4 mm

3 pieces of 20-gauge non-tarnish, antiqued copper wire, each 4 feet (1.2 m) long*

5 feet (1.5 m) of non-tarnish antiqued copper wire, 20-gauge*

$2\frac{5}{8}$ inches (6.7 cm) of 16-gauge copper wire

* The wire lengths are given for a wrist with a 7-inch (17.8 cm) circumference.

TOOLS

Round-nose pliers

Multi-barrel pliers, 6 mm and 8.5 mm in diameter

Chain-nose pliers with nylon-coated jaws (see Note)

Metal hole punch

Dowel, 6 mm (optional)

Vise (optional)

Flush wire cutters

Bracelet mandrel (optional)

Chasing hammer and steel block

DIMENSIONS

Circumference, 7 inches (17.8 cm)

INSTRUCTIONS

Note: Dipping the pliers' jaws into a rubberlike product protects wire from getting scarred by the metal of the tool. Be sure to follow the manufacturer's suggestions.

I Use the punch to make a hole near the stem end of each of the three leaf findings. Use the round-nose pliers to curl the sharp stem ends in.

BRAID

2 Use the tip of the round-nose pliers to make a tight U-bend that is 2 feet (61 cm) from one end of the 5-foot (1.5 m) piece of 20-gauge wire.

3 Hold the three 4-foot (1.2 m) wires together. Wrap the midpoint of these around the 6-mm section of the multi-barrel pliers. Cross the three left-side wires over the three right-side wires.

4 Thread the 5-foot (1.5 m) piece of wire through the loop and hold it to the right side (figure 1).

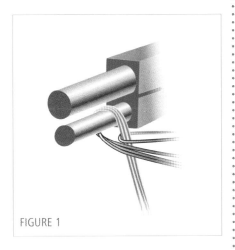

FIGURE 1

5 Holding the paired wires together, side by side, bring them to the left. Cross them over the right-side trio of wires, as shown in figure 2. Bring the three wires on the left side into the middle, across the paired wires.

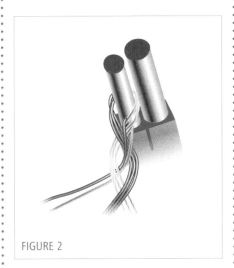

FIGURE 2

6 Continue braiding the groups of wires into an open weave. It may help to put the bracelet's end loop over one end of a dowel held in a vise. Keep the wires in each strand flat and right next to each other. Make the opening spaces in the braid 2 to 3 mm long. Don't pull the wires too tightly.

7 Stop braiding when the braided wire is 1¼ inches (3.2 cm) short of the desired length (including the initial loop) and the two-wire strand is in the center.

LOOP END

8 Wrap the two-wire strand around the three-wire strand it just crossed, then across the other three-wire strand (figure 3).

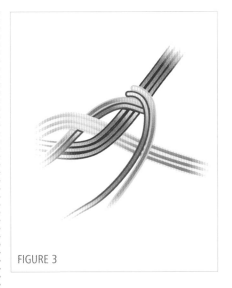

FIGURE 3

9 Wrap the trio that was not wrapped by the wire pair around the large jaw of the multi-barrel pliers. Make a large loop that is in the same plane as the braid. The wires' ends should point back toward the braid and pass underneath the other wires (figure 4).

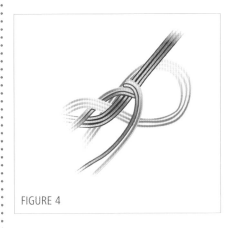

FIGURE 4

10 Bring the *wrapped* three-wire strand around and inside the loop, as shown in figure 5.

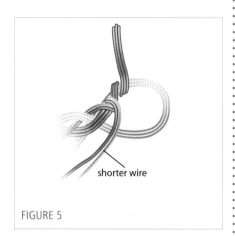

shorter wire

FIGURE 5

11 The two-wire strand is crossing over one side of the loop. Wrap the longer wire once around the side of the loop. Bring it up on the side of the two-wire strand nearer to you, ready to weave back up through the braid. Wrap the shorter wire once around the side of the loop and bring it up on the farther side, ready to coil around the loop.

12 Using the wires that wrapped over the loop, now separately wrap each one around the loop again and to the outside. Bring each one anywhere up through the braid (figure 6). Wrap each wire around any other nearby wire to anchor it. Cut the wire to leave a tail 1 inch (2.5 cm) long.

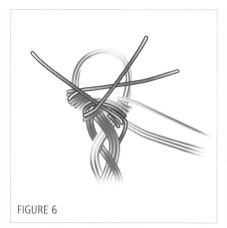

FIGURE 6

FINISH THE LOOP

13 Form each of the 1-inch (2.5 cm) tails into a tight spiral (figure 7).

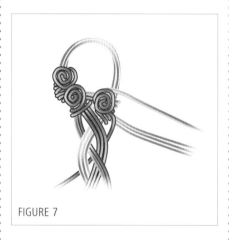

FIGURE 7

14 Coil the shortest wire from the paired strand around the entire loop. Cut the wire to 1 inch (2.5 cm) long and make a tight spiral out of the tail (figure 8).

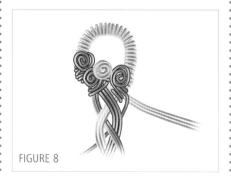

FIGURE 8

15 Weave the longer wire from the two-wire strand back up through the braid until it reaches the first loop you made (figure 9).

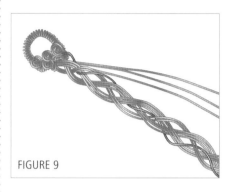

FIGURE 9

16 Coil-wrap the loop with this longer wire, then cut a 1-inch (2.5 cm) tail.

ADD BEADS

17 Using the bracelet mandrel (or other oval-shaped object), shape the bracelet so that the ends have a ¾-inch (1.9 cm) opening between them.

18 Find the center point of the bracelet, where the middle leaf will go. Find the halfway point between the loops' ends and the middle leaf. Plan to position the other two leaves slightly less than halfway between the middle leaf and the loop ends. This will leave enough space to add two crystals between the side leaves and the loop ends.

19 You'll use the remaining three long wires to add the crystals and the leaves. Separate them so you can take each wire through the center of the braid, along a different path, back to the center of the bracelet.

20 Add the first crystal bead to one of the three wires. Secure the bead by weaving its wire parallel to the rest of the braid, then back into the center of the braid. Add another crystal.

21 To add a leaf, pass one of the three wires through the leaf's hole. Hold the leaf at an angle along the braided base. Secure it to the bracelet by bringing the other wires across the leaf too, as shown in figure 10.

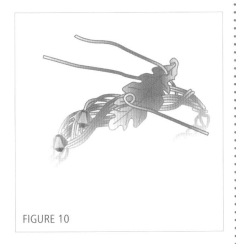

FIGURE 10

22 Add another crystal, then the middle leaf, another crystal, the last leaf, and the last two crystals. After the last crystal, secure each wire by wrapping it around the loop or around part of the braided base. Cut each wire to a 1-inch (2.5 cm) tail. Shape all four of the tails into tight spirals. Adjust the bracelet's overall shape as necessary.

S-CLASP

23 Flatten both ends of the $2\frac{5}{8}$-inch (6.7 cm) wire with the chasing hammer and the block. Make a tiny loop at one end with the tip of the round-nose pliers. Make a tiny loop facing in the other direction at the opposite end. Fashion the clasp with the smaller side of the bail-making pliers so that it's the

size and shape of the template shown in figure 11.

Actual Size

FIGURE 11

24 Flatten both sides of the curves, and the straight wire between them, with the chasing hammer and the block. One side of it should be closed and the other slightly open. Reshape the clasp with your fingers if necessary.

25 Open the closed side of the clasp like a jump ring. Attach the smaller of the bracelet's looped ends to it. Make sure the clasp will be pointing in the right direction!

Charred Polymer Pendant

Designed by GORDON STRICKLAND

The wirework on this piece is like the flight of a loopy ladybug. It will help you learn to handle soft craft wire with confidence.

MATERIALS

1 red and black top-drilled polymer clay bead, 28 x 22 x 12 mm

28 inches (71.1 cm) of silver-plated craft wire, 16 gauge

TOOLS

Round-nose pliers

Chain-nose pliers

Flat-nose pliers

Bent chain-nose pliers

Flush wire cutters

Round, stepped mandrel with 7- and 8-mm diameter options

Chasing hammer and steel block

Needle file

Jeweler's polishing cloth

Toothbrush

Dish soap

DIMENSIONS

1¹⁄₁₆ x 1⁷⁄₈ inches (2.7 x 4.8 cm)

INSTRUCTIONS

1 Cut two pieces of the 16-gauge craft wire, each 14 inches (35.6 cm) long. One will be a bail wire and the other a coil wire. Insert the bail wire through the bead from left to right, exposing 1½ inches (3.8 cm) on the right side of the bead. With the bead face up, fold the wire tightly onto both sides of the bead, crossing the wires at the top, with the shorter end of the wire underneath the longer one.

2 Using the round-nose pliers, bend the long side of the wire so it's flush with the bead top and aligned along the bead's vertical axis (figure 1).

FIGURE 1

3 With the chain-nose pliers (or your fingers), make two closing wraps around the longer wire with the shorter one. Use the cutters to trim the short wire flush in the center of the back of the longer wire. Use the chain-nose pliers to press the trimmed end tightly to the longer wire.

4 Use the 8-mm section of the mandrel to loop the longer wire from the front of the bead toward the back. This loop is the bail (figure 2).

FIGURE 2

5 Use the 7-mm section of the mandrel to form two counterclockwise, concentric loops just to the right of the bail (figure 3).

FIGURE 3

6 Bring the wire around to the back and bottom of the bail, then around to the front, holding the concentric loops tightly in the flat-nose pliers as you do. This stabilizes the loop's shape (figure 4).

FIGURE 4

Charred Polymer Pendant

7 Using the flat of your thumb, vertically line up the wire with the bail. On the opposite side, form an S curve that flows from the top to the right side of the bead, almost to the base, as shown in figure 5.

FIGURE 5

8 Using the tip of the round-nose pliers, form two closed loops barely big enough to let a 16-gauge wire slip through them. The closing loops should be ¹⁄₁₆ inch (1.6 mm) inside the left edge of the bead.

Trim the end of the bail wire at the back of the second loop. This completes the bail wire.

9 Use the bent chain-nose pliers to make a 90° bend ¼ inch (6 mm) from one end of the coil wire. Hold that short wire end in the tool so the longer end of the wire lies flat along the back of the pliers, and use your fingers to shape the longer section of the wire into a four-coil spiral (figure 6).

FIGURE 6

10 Remove the coil from the pliers. Use the cutters to trim the short end of the wire at the spiral's center.

11 While it's facing down on the steel block, flatten the spiral with a chasing hammer. Then, with the spirals clockwise and face up, insert the end of the coil wire through the binding loops of the bail wire. The spiral should lie flush against the base of the S curve (figure 7).

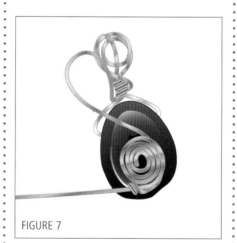
FIGURE 7

12 Holding the coil and S curve together and pressed against the bead, bend the wire to the back of the bead, horizontally across the back, and to just past the halfway point on the side.

13 Bend the wire up 90°, to the top of the bead. The wire should lie in front of the bail wire where the bail wire exits the bead on that side. Make two tight loops around the base of the bail.

14 Trim the remaining tail of the coil wire to 1 inch (2.5 cm) and flatten the last ¼ inch (6 mm) with the chasing hammer. Use the file to round the cut end and remove any burrs.

15 Using straight chain-nose pliers, create a loose counterclockwise spiral (two rounds) with this filed end. Press it flat to the bead. (*Note*: Use straight chain-nose pliers and light pressure to smooth loose spirals and curves. Round-nose pliers tend to kink and dent soft wire.)

16 With a jeweler's cloth, clean all of the surfaces of the pendant. Then with a toothbrush, dish soap, and warm water, wash the pendant to remove any residue.

Back view

Pearl Earrings

Practice your wrapped bead loops by making lustrous clusters of green freshwater pearls.

Designed by MARIE CASTIGLIA

MATERIALS

16 freshwater pearls, 4 mm

16 gold-filled head pins, 22 gauge, each 2 inches (5.1 cm) long

1 pair of gold-filled French ear wires

TOOLS

Round-nose pliers

Flat-nose pliers

Flush wire cutters

DIMENSIONS

Length, 1⅛ inches (2.9 cm)

INSTRUCTIONS

1 Slide a pearl onto a head pin.

2 With the round-nose pliers, make a loop in the head pin just above the pearl.

3 Feed the loop in the base of the ear wire to the inside of the loop you made.

4 Wrap the tail of the head pin around the loop two more times.

5 Trim the excess wire with the flush wire cutters.

6 Repeat steps 1–5 until you have eight wrapped bead loops on each ear wire.

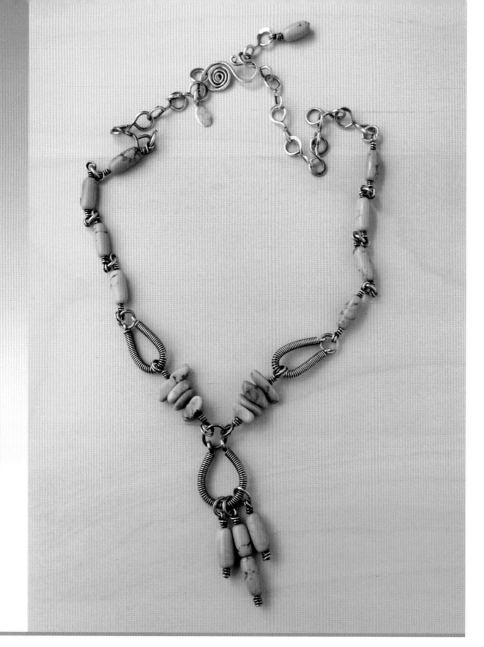

MATERIALS

8 side-drilled turquoise nuggets, 9 to 14 mm long

13 turquoise tube beads, 5 x 12 mm

2 pieces of round sterling silver wire, 20 gauge, each 8 inches (20.3 cm) long

12 pieces of round sterling silver wire, 20 gauge, each 6 inches (15.2 cm) long

72 inches (1.8 m) of sterling silver wire, 24 gauge

3 pieces of round sterling silver wire, 16 gauge, each 2¾ inches (7 cm) long

4¼ inches (10.8 cm) of sterling silver wire, 16 gauge

8 sterling silver jump rings, 16 gauge, 6 mm

1 sterling silver jump ring, 16 gauge, 10 mm

5 sterling silver jump rings, 16 gauge, 8 mm

13 pieces of sterling silver wire, 16 gauge, each 1½ inches (3.8 cm) long

TOOLS

Round-nose pliers

Bent-nose pliers

Multi-barrel pliers with 12-mm and 8-mm circumferences

2 pairs of flat-nose pliers

Flush wire cutters

Wire-coiling tool with 2-mm mandrel

Chasing hammer and steel block

Liver of sulfur gel

Steel wool, grade 0000

DIMENSIONS

Length, 24 inches (61 cm)

Designed by BARBRA DAVIS

Nuggets
Necklace

Update the turquoise-and-silver classic—and show off all your wireworking skills—with this gorgeous necklace.

INSTRUCTIONS

NUGGET LINKS

1 Position one end of an 8-inch piece of 20-gauge wire ½ inch (1.3 cm) at the place on the round-nose pliers that will make a 4-mm inner diameter loop. Make a double-loop wrap. Slide on four of the turquoise nuggets, then finish the link with another double-loop wrap (figure 1). Repeat the process to make another Nugget Link with the other four nuggets. Set aside.

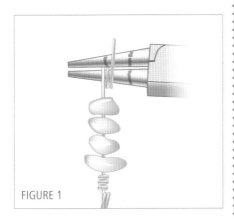

FIGURE 1

KNOTTED HEAD PINS

2 With the bent-nose pliers, make a sharp bend 1 inch (2.5 cm) from the end of one of the 6-inch (15.2 cm) 20-gauge wires. Squeeze the tip of the folded wire tightly with the bent-nose pliers.

3 On the 1-inch (2.5 cm) side of the wire, make another bend ¼ inch (6 mm) down (figure 2). Holding the tip of the

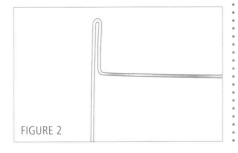

FIGURE 2

wire with the bent-nose pliers, wrap the bent-wire section around the paired wire section, down to the tip of the wire fold (figure 3). Cut the excess wire with the flush wire cutters. Adjust the knot as needed with the bent-nose pliers. Make two more of these Knotted Head Pins.

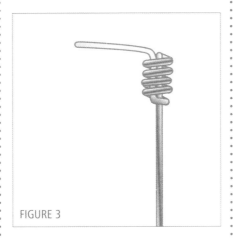

FIGURE 3

FRINGE-BEAD DANGLES

4 Slide a tube bead onto one of the Knotted Head Pins made in step 3. Finish the element with a double-loop wrap. Make another dangle with a single bead, and then make a third dangle with two beads (figure 4).

FIGURE 4

5 To make the bead dangle for the back of the necklace, use a 6-inch (15.2 cm) length of the 20-gauge wire. Slide a tube bead onto it about halfway down. Press one end of the wire along the

length of the bead, then wrap it tightly around the wire at the other end several times. Cut the wire and tuck it in. With the remaining wire end, make a double wrapped loop.

TUBE BEAD LINKS

6 Using one of the remaining eight lengths of 6-inch (15.2 cm) 20-gauge wires and the round-nose pliers, make a double-loop wrap with a triple-wrapped shank. Slide on a tube bead, cut the excess wire, and tuck in the wire end with bent-nose pliers. Make another triple-wrapped-shank double loop on the other end of the bead. This makes one Tube Bead Link. Repeat this step with the seven remaining turquoise tube beads and the seven remaining 6-inch (15.2 cm) 20-gauge wires.

7 Connect four of the Tube Bead Links with three of the 6-mm sterling silver jump rings. Repeat the connection process for the other four Tube Bead Links.

U-LINKS

8 Use the 2-mm mandrel on the wire-coiling tool to coil the 72-inch (1.8 m) piece of 24-gauge wire. Cut the coil into three Coiled Lengths, each 1¾ inches (4.4 cm) long.

9 Slide one of the Coiled Lengths made in step 8 onto one of the 2¾-inch (7 cm) pieces of 16-gauge wire. Hold one end of the straight wire ⅛ inch (3 mm) in the end of the round-nose pliers and make a simple loop. Do the same at the other end. Using the 12-mm barrel of the multi-barrel pliers, bend the Coiled Length into a large U-link. Make two smaller U-links with the 8-mm barrel.

ASSEMBLY

10 Attach an 8-mm jump ring to each Dangle, then slide them all onto the larger U-link you made in step 9.

11 Use your bent-nose and flat-nose pliers to open the 10-mm jump ring. Slide it through the simple loops at the top of the larger U-link you made in step 9. Before closing the jump ring, add both of the Nugget Links made in step 1.

12 Slip one of the smaller U-links through the double-wrapped loop on one end of a Nugget Link. Join the other smaller U-link and Nugget Link in the same way.

13 Slip an opened 8-mm jump ring through the simple loops on one of the smaller U-links made in step 9. Before you close the jump ring, add the connected Tube Bead Link completed in step 6. Connect the other smaller U-Link and Tube Bead Link in the same way.

CHAIN LINKS

14 Mark one jaw of the round-nose pliers, so you can use it to make simple loops with 4-mm and 6-mm inner diameters. You'll form the first Chain Link from one of the 1½-inch (3.8 cm) wires by making a simple loop at each end. After you make the first loop, hold the wire by the loop. Turn a loop in the other end of the wire that is perpendicular to the first loop. Make 12 more links this way.

15 Use the round-nose pliers to center all the loops directly over their wires.

16 Use the chasing hammer and steel block to flatten and strengthen the loop ends on all 13 links.

FINAL CONNECTIONS

17 Attach the two remaining 6-mm jump rings to the ends of both Tube Bead Links. Attach five of the Chain Links to the 6-mm jump rings by opening one end like a jump ring. Attach eight Chain Links to the other side in the same way.

18 Starting at one end of a 4¼-inch (10.8 cm) piece of 16-gauge wire, use the round-nose pliers to form the first three turns of a spiral. Make a sharp bend in the fourth turn, and finish forming the rest of the spiral. Make a tiny loop at the tip of the other wire end that faces the spiral.

19 Using the 12-mm jaw of the multi-barrel pliers, form the other end of the wire into a large curve in the direction opposite the four-turn spiral you made in step 18 (figure 5).

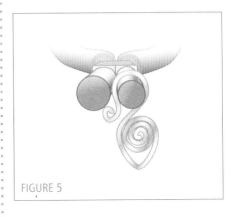

FIGURE 5

20 Use a chasing hammer and a steel block to flatten and strengthen the clasp.

21 Use the liver of sulfur gel on the silver wire to darken it; avoid the turquoise. Wash and dry the piece as directed by the manufacturer. Give the silver a final buff with the fine steel wool to remove some of the patina.

Black Bead Bracelet

Neatly wrapped bead loops let you join glossy faceted rounds with daisy spacers and bright trios of tiny, iridescent bicones in this sparkling design.

Designed by KAMMY PIETRASZEK

MATERIALS

6 padparadscha AB bicone beads, 4 mm

6 smoky quartz bicone beads, 4 mm

6 fuchsia AB bicone beads, 4 mm

14 gold vermeil daisy spacers, 4 mm

7 round faceted black glass beads, 12 mm

7 pieces of half-hard gold-filled wire, 24 gauge, each 3 inches (8 cm) long

18 gold-filled head pins, 24 gauge, 1 inch (2.5 cm)

6 gold-filled closed jump rings, 6 mm

1 gold-filled toggle clasp with a 14-mm-diameter clasp and a 24-mm bar

TOOLS

Chain-nose pliers

Round-nose pliers

Flush wire cutters

Permanent marker

Wooden dowels, ¼ inch (6 mm) and ⁵⁄₁₆ inch (8 mm) in diameter

Ball-peen hammer and steel block

Jeweler's file

Liver of sulfur

Steel wool, grade 0000

Tweezers

Pretreated polishing pad

DIMENSIONS

Length, 8⅜ inches (21.3 cm)

Black Bead Bracelet

INSTRUCTIONS

1 Make six padparadscha AB bicone drops: string one bicone bead onto a head pin. Create a simple loop that fits snugly above the bead with round-nose pliers. Trim the head pin to within ¼ inch (6 mm) of the bead with flush wire cutters. Press the cut end into the wrap with the chain-nose pliers.

2 Make six 4-mm smoky quartz bicone drops, using the method described in step 1. Make six 4-mm fuchsia bicone drops in the same way.

3 Use the permanent marker to mark ¼ inch (6 mm) from the tip of a jaw of the round-nose pliers. You'll use this mark to create loops of a consistent size for the links of your bracelet.

4 Starting 1 inch (2.5 cm) from the end of one of the 3-inch (7.6 cm) wires, bend it at a 90° angle into an L shape. Use the round-nose pliers to half-turn the shorter end of the L shape. Slip a closed jump ring onto the half-loop. Finish the loop with three wire wraps (figure 1). Snip the excess wire with the cutters. Use the chain-nose pliers to pinch the wire's end into the bottom of the wrapped section.

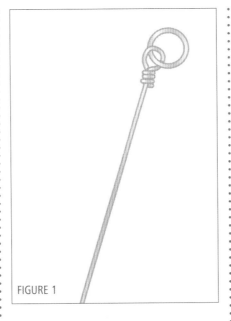

FIGURE 1

5 String one daisy spacer, one black bead, then another daisy spacer onto the open end of the wire you worked with in step 4. Create a second loop with round-nose pliers, leaving ⅛ inch (3 mm) of wire between the spacer and the loop. Add another closed jump ring to this loop, then wrap it closed. Snip the excess wire with the cutters. This is a wrapped bead link.

6 Repeat steps 4 and 5, connecting beaded links with closed jump rings until you have connected seven bead links with six jump rings. There should

be a beaded link on either end of the unit. Keep the last loops on either end of the bracelet open (figure 2).

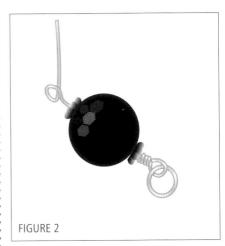

FIGURE 2

7 Attach one padparadscha bicone drop, one smoky quartz bicone drop, and one fuchsia bicone drop to one of the six closed jump rings, for a total of three drops per jump ring. Repeat this process for the five remaining jump rings.

8 Attach the two parts of the toggle clasp to the open loop ends, then close them around the clasp's connector rings by wrapping the loops.

MATERIALS

6 drilled Peruvian amazonite nuggets, 28–30 mm long

8–12 amazonite chips

32 inches (81.3 cm) of 22-gauge copper wire

8 inches (20.3 cm) of 16-gauge copper wire

4 inches (10.2 cm) of 18-gauge copper wire

TOOLS

Round-nose pliers

Flush wire cutters

Diamond file

Ball-peen hammer and steel block

Rubber mallet (optional)

DIMENSIONS

Length, 7¾ inches (19.7 cm)

Designed by **DIANE MABREY**

Amazonite-Copper Bracelet

Bold and chunky Peruvian gemstones are complemented by copper wire in this striking look.

Amazonite-Copper Bracelet

INSTRUCTIONS

Note: File all cut wire ends with the diamond file.

NUGGET STRANDS

1 Check to make sure your wire can pass through the drilled nuggets. Cut one 3½-inch (8.9 cm) piece of the 22-gauge copper wire for each nugget.

2 Make bead loop links for each of three nuggets, linking them together into one Nugget Strand.

3 Make a second strand with three more wire-wrapped nuggets.

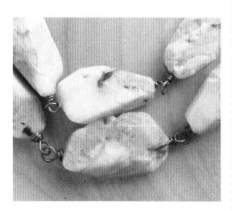

DOUBLE SPIRALS

4 Cut two 4-inch (10.2 cm) pieces of the 16-gauge copper wire.

5 Use the round-nose pliers to make a simple loop at the end of one of the 4-inch (10.2 cm) wires you cut in step 4 (figure 1). Reposition the pliers inside the loop. Firmly holding the wire a little past the midpoint, turn that half of the wire into a spiral (figure 2). Make a slightly larger spiral at the other end of the wire (figure 3). Make another Double Spiral with the other piece of 16-gauge wire.

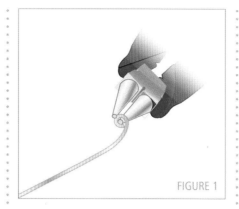

FIGURE 1

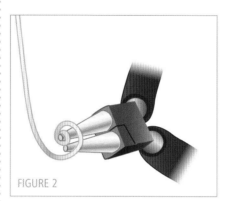

FIGURE 2

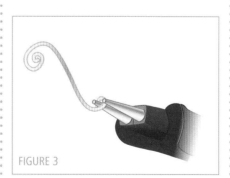

FIGURE 3

6 Hammer each Double Spiral flat and smooth with the ball-peen hammer on the steel block. For added strength, hammer them a bit more with the rubber mallet.

BEAD LOOP LINKS

7 Cut four 3-inch (7.6 cm) pieces of the 22-gauge wire. With these wires, you'll create four bead loop links with a pair of amazonite chips in each one. Make

each link with the round-nose pliers, connecting one of its wrapped loops to a Nugget Strand and the other wrapped loop to the outermost turn in a Double Spiral. Use another bead loop link to connect the other Nugget Strand to the same spiral.

8 Use the other two bead loop links to connect the free ends of the Nugget Strands to the other Double Spiral, as you did in step 7.

CLASP

9 Use the 18-gauge copper wire for the clasp's hook. Mark the halfway point on the wire. Use the tip of the round-nose pliers to fold the wire in half so the cut ends lie snugly side by side.

10 Grasping the pair of cut ends with the pliers' tips, turn them a half-loop. Hook the half-loop into the smaller end of one of the Double Spirals. Hold the half-loop sideways in the pliers so you can close it fully. Turn the loop enough so that the wire ends overlap slightly.

11 Shift the pliers to the midpoint of the straight section. Use a larger section of the pliers' jaws to curve the doubled wire back on itself. Use the tip of the pliers to turn the folded end of the clasp's hook up slightly.

Designed by **RICHELLE HAWKS**

Triple Cherry Hoops

Don't take off for Vegas without these big brassy good-luck earbobs if you want to be sure to hit the cherries, big time.

MATERIALS

36 faceted ruby glass rondelle beads, 4 mm

2 pieces of copper wire, 20 gauge, each 8 inches (20.3 cm) long

2 pieces of copper wire, 20 gauge, each 5½ inches (14 cm) long

2 pieces of copper wire, 20 gauge, each 4¾ inches (12.1 cm) long

2 pieces of copper wire, 20 gauge, each 3½ inches (8.9 cm) long

6 pieces of copper wire, 24 gauge, each 18 inches (45.7 cm) long

2 pieces of copper wire, 20 gauge, each 1¼ inches (3.2 cm) long

TOOLS

Round-nose pliers

Flush wire cutters

Ball-peen hammer and steel block

Jeweler's file

Jeweler's "wire rounder" burr tool or emery board/fine nail file

DIMENSIONS

Diameter, 2¹¹⁄₁₆ inches (6.8 cm)

Triple Cherry Hoops

INSTRUCTIONS

Note: File both ends of the all the wires until they are smooth and rounded. Re-file any trimmed ends as needed.

OUTER HOOPS

I Use the round-nose pliers to make a small loop at one end of an 8-inch (20.3 cm) wire. Use your fingers to form the length of wire into a round hoop shape. Make another small loop at the other end of the wire.

2 Adjust the hoop with your fingers so that both loops match up. The hoop's diameter should be 2½ inches (6.4 cm) across.

3 Place the hoop flat on the steel block and use the ball end of the hammer to create texture on the entire surface of this side of the hoop. When the wire starts to curl off the block, flip the hoop over and lightly tap with the flat side of the hammer until it's flattened. (You will likely need to hammer both sides three or four times each to get enough texture and still keep the hoop from curling too much.) Shape the hoop back into a circle with your fingers, and make sure the loops match up again.

4 Repeat steps 1–3 for the other earring.

INNER HOOPS

5 Shape each of the 5½-inch (14 cm), 4¾-inch (12.1 cm), and 3½-inch (8.9 cm) wires into circles. Repeat step 3 to add texture to them.

6 After hammering the wires, use your fingers to reshape and overlap their ends enough so they sit snugly side by side (figure 1).

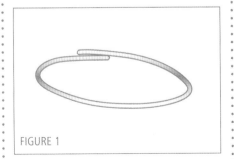

FIGURE 1

7 Place the largest of the three inner hoops so that its overlapped ends are at 8 o'clock on the outer hoop.

8 Leaving a 1½-inch (3.8 cm) starting tail, tightly wrap them together there with a piece of the 18-inch (45.7 cm) wire. Make sure you wrap the overlapped ends of the inner loop, crisscrossing it as you go. Also be sure to pass directly over the place you began the wrapping, to secure the end of the wire.

9 After a dozen or so wraps, string a ruby bead onto the wrapping wire. Wrap the wire tightly around the two hoops once. Add five more of the beads in the same way. They should all face outward in a cluster. As you work, be sure to wrap between the beads in order to secure them.

10 To finish the wrap, find a stopping place and feed the end of the wire under a wrap. Pull it gently but snugly (figure 2), snip the tail to ¾ inch (2 cm), and file the end. Use a jaw of the round-nose pliers as a mandrel for a decorative coil. Push the coil in with the end of the pliers' handle if desired. Do the same with the other tail.

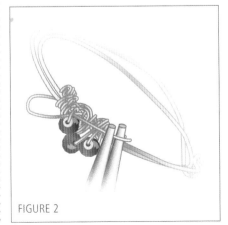

FIGURE 2

11 Place the medium-size inner hoop so that its overlapped ends are at 2 o'clock on the outer hoop. As you do so, catch the larger inner hoop inside the medium one (figure 3). Repeat steps 8–10.

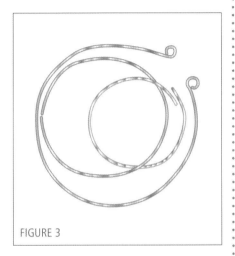

FIGURE 3

12 Place the overlapped ends of the smallest inner hoop at 8 o'clock. Catch the first inner hoop inside it. Repeat steps 8–10.

ADJUSTMENTS

13 All the hoops now form a single component, but you'll notice there is some give. Use your fingers to round the whole component as necessary and make sure the loops of the outer hoop match up. Push them together and work with that tension so that they line up straight when they are ½ inch (1.3 cm) apart.

14 Grasp one of the outer hoops' loops with the pliers and twist it so it's at a 90° angle to the component. Twist one to the left and the other to the right. Do the same for the other earring.

15 Use the pliers to tighten and close the loops completely, with no gaps between the end of the wire and the loop base. Overlap the loops' wire ends if necessary. These loops will serve as the ear wire connections. You have now finished the component for the right earring.

EAR WIRES

Note: File the ends of the ear wires until they are very smooth and rounded. Final touches with a jeweler's wire rounder or fine nail file will ensure that the earrings are comfortable to put on.

16 Use the 1½-inch (3.8 cm) piece of filed 20-gauge copper wire to form the ear wires. Make a loop, using the round-nose pliers, on one end of one of the wire pieces.

17 Use your fingers to shape a low arc between the wire's ends. You may want to keep the loop in the pliers' grip while you do so.

18 Attach an ear wire to the right loop at the top of the right earring component using the round-nose pliers. Put the back of it through the left loop and work with the tension of the hoop so that the back end of the ear wire catches the other ear wire loop. Use the round-nose pliers to slightly pull up on the end of the wire, gently, while it's connected through the ear-wire loop of the hoop. Try the earring on to help determine what additional adjustments might need to be made.

19 To make the left earring, follow the same steps but reverse the placements of the inner loop connections and wire wrapping so that it forms a mirror image. That is, the 8 o'clock connections should be placed at 4 o'clock, and the 2 o'clock connection should be placed at 10 o'clock. The ear wire should be placed with its loop on the left loop at the top of the hoop.

MATERIALS

2 undrilled double-terminated quartz beads, 7 x 3.5 mm

2 pieces of 14-karat gold–filled round half-hard wire, 21 gauge, each 1⅝ inches (4.1 cm) long

2 pieces of 14-karat gold–filled round half-hard wire, 21 gauge, each 2 inches (5.1 cm) long

6¾ inches (17.1 cm) of 14-karat gold–filled round dead-soft wire, 21 gauge

TOOLS

Round-nose pliers

Flat-nose pliers

Mandrel, ¾ inch (2 cm) in diameter

Chasing hammer and steel block

Needle file

Dowel, ¼ inch (6 mm) in diameter

Side flush wire cutters

DIMENSIONS

Length, 1 inch (2.5 cm)

Designed by YUKO MACHIDA

Double-pointed quartz is taken to a new height of style when it's gently bound in a gold wire cage.

Quartz "Diamond" Earrings

INSTRUCTIONS

EAR WIRES

1 Using the round-nose pliers, make a loop at one end of a 1⅝-inch (4.1 cm) wire.

2 Lay the wire on the mandrel and curve the wire away from your little loop.

3 Using a chasing hammer, gently hammer the ear wires on the block to harden them.

4 File any rough edges on the end, and gently turn it up with the pliers (figure 1).

FIGURE 1

5 Repeat steps 1–4 for the other ear wire.

HOOPS

6 Wrap one of the 2-inch (5 cm) wires around the mandrel.

7 Remove the curved wire from the mandrel and use the round-nose pliers to make an inward-facing simple loop on each end of it.

8 Using a chasing hammer, gently flatten the hoops on the block with the hammer to harden them.

9 Repeat steps 1–3 for the other hoop.

FINISHING

10 Coil the 6¾-inch (17.1 cm) wire 10 times around the dowel.

11 Cut the coil in the center so that you have two coiled wires of equal length (figure 2). Remove the wire from the dowel.

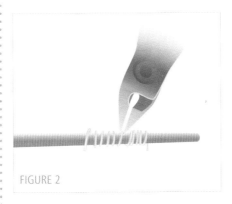

FIGURE 2

12 Use the round-nose pliers to make a tiny loop at the end of each coil.

13 Unwind a coil just enough to fit one of the quartz pieces in the center of it. Re-tighten the coil so the quartz is firmly held inside it.

14 Attach the coil ends to the hoop by the tiny loops you made in step 12.

15 Repeat steps 13 and 14 to finish the other earring.

16 Open the simple loop on one of the ear wires, as you would a jump ring. Slip it through the tiny loop you made in step 12, then close it. Do the same for the other earring.

MATERIALS

- 2 iridescent gold faceted glass teardrop beads, 14 mm
- 2 iridescent gold faceted glass teardrop beads, 11 mm
- 2 iridescent gold faceted glass teardrop beads, 8 mm
- 2 multicolor vintage round lamp work beads, 10 mm
- 2 pieces of steel wire, 19 gauge, each 13 inches (33 cm) long
- 2 pieces of steel wire, 24 gauge, each 22 inches (55.9 cm) long
- 2 pieces of steel wire, 24 gauge, each 5 inches (12.7 cm) long
- 6 small claw-style oxidized brass bead caps
- 2 flat oxidized brass bead caps
- 2 disk-style oxidized brass bead caps
- 1 pair of oxidized brass ear wires

TOOLS

Round-nose pliers

Flush wire cutters

Cotton cloth

Jeweler's file

Microcrystalline wax

Cotton swabs

DIMENSIONS

Length, 4⅛ inches (10.5 cm)

Designed by RICHELLE HAWKS

Create carefree bohemian style when you wrap nonconformist steel wire around (and around) glowing golden teardrop beads.

Boho Teardrop Earrings

INSTRUCTIONS

Note: Before you work with the steel wire, clean the carbon off of it with the cloth. Use the jeweler's file to smooth and round one end of each cut piece. Seal all of the cleaned and filed wires with a light application of the wax, using a cotton swab.

ROSE MEDALLIONS

1 Using the round-nose pliers, make a tight loop at the filed end of one of the 19-gauge wires. This will be the center-top portion of the rose medallion.

2 Move the pliers ¼ inch (6 mm) away from the loop, and use your free hand to turn the length of the wire at a sharp angle so that a larger curve is created directly under the first loop (figure 1).

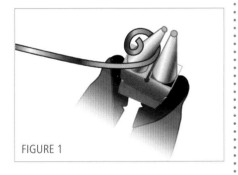

FIGURE 1

3 Continue to shape the rose medallion, varying slightly the angle and how far you move the pliers from the last angle you formed. Aim for a freeform but generally round final rose shape.

4 When the rose is 1 inch (2.5 cm) in diameter, use the cutters to trim any excess off the working end. Use the file to smooth and round the end.

5 Finish the end by coiling it into a fairly tight loop in the middle of the back.

Push it in lightly with the end of the pliers' handle.

6 Repeat steps 1–5 to form a second rose of the same general shape and size.

7 Consider the shapes and determine which areas of each rose medallion will be the top and bottom, for attachments. Set the medallions aside in those positions.

BEAD STACK

8 Clean and lightly seal one of the 22-inch (55.9 cm) pieces of the 24-gauge steel wire with the wax. File one end of the wire until it's smooth and rounded.

9 Starting 7 inches (17.8 cm) from the filed end, make two very tight side-by-side loops with the tip of the pliers (figure 2).

FIGURE 2

10 Hold the double loops together, across their widths, with the round-nose pliers. Tightly wrap the shorter end of wire around the base of the two loops. To make the bead stack, string the following elements onto the longer wire:

- a claw-style bead cap
- a flat bead cap
- a 14-mm teardrop bead
- an 11-mm teardrop bead
- an 8-mm teardrop bead

11 Use the round-nose pliers to attach the bead stack to the bottom of one of the rose medallions with a simple wrapped loop. Instead of finishing off the wrapped loop, continue wrapping the wire down the bead stack. Cross the wire against the top bead at a slight angle and wrap it a couple of times laterally between the top and the middle bead.

12 Continue to wrap the wire down, crossing the middle and bottom beads at the same angle as the top bead, as well as between them. Wrap the wire a couple of times at the bottom over the last bead cap.

13 Use the cutters to trim this piece of wire ½ inch (1.3 cm) from the base near the bead cap. File the end until smooth. Bring the end around the bead cap and press in the very tip.

14 You'll use the wire that was left at the bottom to wrap the stack upward now. To start, cover up the pressed-in tip of the other wire end by wrapping directly over it. Then work your way up the stack as before: cross the beads with the wire and wrap it between beads. You might need to grasp the stack's bottom loops with the pliers before you start wrapping.

15 Wrap the remaining wire around the top of the loop and press the end slightly to finish.

16 Repeat steps 8–15 to form the other Bead Stack.

TOP COMPONENT

17 Starting 2 inches (5 cm) from an end of one of the 5-inch (17.9 cm) wires, make a loop. Hold the loop in the pliers and

wrap the tail once around the loop to secure it. This will be the top of the ear wire attachment. Leave the remaining length of the wire unwrapped for now.

18 To make the top component, string the following elements onto the wire:

- a claw-style bead cap
- a lamp work bead
- a disk-style bead cap
- a claw-style bead cap

19 Use the round-nose pliers to make a loop. Slip the beaded component onto the open wire at the top of the rose medallion. Wrap the remaining wire over the bead cap. Use the pliers' handle to press the tip inward.

20 Return to the top loop and finish by wrapping the remaining wire under the loop and around the bead cap to secure, then finish by pressing the tip inward.

21 Attach an ear wire. Using the cloth, carefully go over the steel wire to clean any remaining carbon from the steel. Apply a bit more microcrystalline wax, using a cotton swab, for a final seal. Remove any wax remnants from the beads, using a clean swab if necessary.

22 Repeat steps 17–21 to form the Top Component for the second earring.

MATERIALS

10 pale pink smooth glass beads with silver metal cores, 4 mm

2 raspberry center-drilled, Czech pressed center glass drops, 12 x 10 mm

2 metallic black bicone beads, 4 mm

2 pieces of 20-gauge gunmetal wire, 2 inches (5 cm) long

12 gunmetal balled head pins, 24 gauge, 2 inches (5 cm) long

2 etched jump rings, 16 gauge, 12 mm

TOOLS

Round-nose pliers

Bent-nose pliers

2 pairs of flat-nose pliers

Flush wire cutters

Needle file

Stepped mandrel

Jeweler's hammer and steel block

DIMENSIONS

Length, 1¹³⁄₁₆ inches (4.6 cm)

Designed by **NANCY SCOTT** and **LAURA B. SCOTT**

Raspberry Tart Earrings

This tarty little design plants luscious berry-colored glass melon drops amid pink glass dangles and hand-forged ear wires.

Raspberry Tart Earrings

INSTRUCTIONS

WRAPPED BEAD LOOPS

1 Make wrapped bead loops from the 10 pink glass beads and 10 of the 24-gauge head pins. Slip a pink glass bead onto each head pin. Use the round-nose pliers to turn a simple loop with a tail in each pin. Use the flat-nose pliers to wrap the base of each loop with the tail.

2 Trim any excess wire with the cutters. Use the bent-nose pliers to tuck the tail of each cut wire tightly against the wrapped bead loop (figure 1).

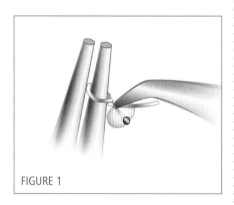

FIGURE 1

3 Slide a raspberry drop bead onto one of the remaining head pins. Add a metallic bicone to the head pin. Close with a wrapped bead loop. Make a second wrapped bead loop with the other raspberry drop, metallic bicone, and head pin.

FRENCH EAR WIRES

4 File the ends of the wires smooth with the file. Bend the tip of each wire with the round-nose pliers to form a loop.

5 Hold the wire with the loop facing up. Bend the wire against the mandrel, applying the pressure of your thumb on the wire from the center out (figure 2).

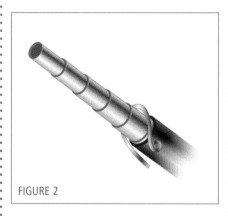

FIGURE 2

6 Use the flat-nose pliers to add a small bend to the end of the earrings.

7 Make the bend level with the loop at the other end (figure 3).

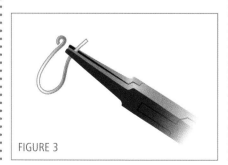

FIGURE 3

8 Using a flat hammer and the steel block, flatten the section of the ear wire between the curve and the loop.

FINAL CONNECTIONS

9 Open the etched jump ring and slide on the following:

- 3 pink glass wrapped loops
- 1 raspberry-drop wrapped loops
- 2 more pink glass wrapped loops
- an ear wire

10 Close the jump ring.

11 Repeat steps 9 and 10 for the other earring.

MATERIALS

65 freshwater pearls, 4 mm

16 inches (40.6 cm) of 4- or 5-mm open-link sterling silver chain

1 lobster-style sterling silver clasp, 12 mm

2 open jump rings, 16 gauge, 5 mm

5 open jump rings, 16 gauge, 6 mm

65 ball-tip silver head pins, 24 gauge, each 1½ inches (3.8 cm) long

TOOLS

2 pairs of flat-nose pliers

Round-nose pliers

Bent-nose pliers

Liver of sulfur

Polishing cloth

Flush wire cutters

DIMENSIONS

Length, 16¾ inches (42.5 cm)

INSTRUCTIONS

1 Apply the liver of sulfur to all of the metal components.

2 Attach the lobster-style clasp to the ends of the chain with the 5-mm open jump rings. Be sure to open the jump rings firmly with two pairs of pliers. As you close the jump ring, move the pliers back and forth several times, to harden the metal.

Designed by **SHARON CLANCY**

These dramatic pearl clusters seem almost to float, thanks to the simple, lightweight chain.

Dark Pearls Necklace

Dark Pearls Necklace

3 Buff the chain and clasp with the polishing cloth. Do this very gently to let only the raised surfaces of the metal shine through the dark patina. It's important to buff the chain before attaching the pearls.

4 Place one pearl onto each of the head pins. Make a closed loop for each pearl by bending the wire toward you with the flat-nose pliers, gripping it just above the pearl. Use the round-nose pliers to grip the bent portion of the head pin. Wrap the wire away from you, around the top jaw of the pliers. Insert the bottom jaw into the loop that you just wrapped. Use the bent-nose pliers to close the loop and wrap it several times (figure 1). Cut any excess wire, and crimp down any sharp edges with your bent-nose pliers.

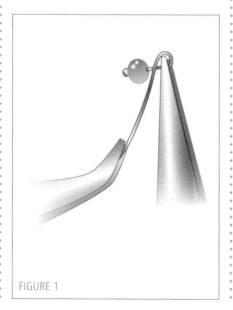

FIGURE 1

5 Use two pairs of pliers to open one of the 6-mm jump rings. Place 13 of the wrapped pearls onto it, then attach the cluster to the midpoint of the chain. Close the jump ring.

6 Attach the other four clusters to the chain, spacing them 1¼ inches (3.2 cm) apart, along either side of the central cluster.

Designed by **NATHALIE MORNU**

Azure Cloisonné Earrings

Gold-veined enamel beads dance at the end
of delicate chain "suspenders."

MATERIALS

4 round glass beads, 7 mm

4 vermeil disks, 8 mm

2 cloisonné beads, 13 mm

8 inches (20.3 cm) of 20-gauge gold-filled wire

6 inches (15.2 cm) of fine golden chain

2 jump rings, 5 mm

1 pair of golden ear wires

TOOLS

2 pairs of flat-nose pliers

Round-nose pliers

Flush wire cutters

Tape measure

Permanent marker

DIMENSIONS

Length, 2⅞ inches (7.3 cm)

INSTRUCTIONS

Note: Make both earrings at the same time to shape them identically.

1 Cut the wire in half. String beads onto each piece in this order: glass, vermeil, cloisonné, vermeil, glass.

2 Center the beads on each piece of wire, then bend the wire up in a pleasing arc. Make sure the curvature of both arcs matches. The wire tails sticking out beyond the beads probably won't be the same length—don't worry about it. You have more wire than you need.

3 Mark each of the four wire tails ⅞ inch (2.2 cm) from where it extends beyond the beads. Trim off any extra wire. On each tail, mark ¼ inch (6 mm) from the end, and on that spot, use one of the flat-nose pliers make a 90° bend with the end of the tail pointing outward. Starting at the bend in each of the tails, make a loop that faces in. You've finished making the bottom elements. Set them aside.

4 Cut some chain 1¼ inches (3.2 cm) long. Count the number of links in it. Cut three more pieces of chain containing the same amount of links.

5 Catch one end of chain in either of the loops on a bottom element. Repeat so a piece of chain is caught in each of the loops.

6 Open a jump ring. Catch the ends of both pieces of chain hanging from one bottom element in it, and then add an ear wire. Close the loop. Repeat to finish the other earring.

Teardrops & Maille Necklace

Glowing pear teardrops plus hammered brass look flat-out gorgeous in this maille-inspired design.

Designed by INNA GOR

MATERIALS

- 3 smoky topaz Czech pear teardrops, 14 x 5 mm
- 4 pieces of half-hard round brass wire, 16 gauge, each 2¼ inches (5.7 cm) long
- 4 pieces of half-hard round brass wire, 16 gauge, each 2⅛ inches (5.4 cm) long
- 5½ inches (14 cm) of half-hard round brass wire, 16 gauge
- 3 pieces of dead-soft round brass wire, 24 gauge, each 8 inches (20 cm) long
- 2 pieces of antique bronze cross chain, 1 x 3 x 4 mm, each 5 inches (13 cm) long
- 14 half-hard antique-bronze open jump rings, 20 gauge, 4 mm inner diameter

TOOLS

Round-nose pliers

Chain-nose pliers

2 pairs of flat-nose pliers

Stepped round-nose pliers with 5-, 7-, and 10-mm diameter barrels

Permanent marker

#2 needle file

Round mandrel, 15 mm in diameter

Hammer and steel block or anvil

Flush wire cutters

Tumbler with stainless steel shot mix

Dishwashing liquid

Brown metal-darkening solution for brass and copper

Jewelry polishing cloth

DIMENSIONS

Length, 15¾ inches (40 cm)

INSTRUCTIONS

ARCHED WIRES

1 To aid the assembling process, mark the four longer pieces of the 16-gauge wire with a permanent marker.

2 Smooth all the sharp ends of the wires with the needle file.

3 Form all of the wires into shallow U-shaped arches over the mandrel.

4 Use some scrap wire to practice making 3-mm loops with the round-nose pliers. Mark the jaw of the pliers at that point, so that all your loops will be the same size.

5 Position one of the wires at the mark on the round-nose pliers. Form a loop at each end (figure 1). Repeat the process for all eight 16-gauge pieces.

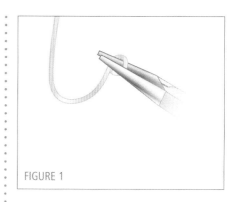

FIGURE 1

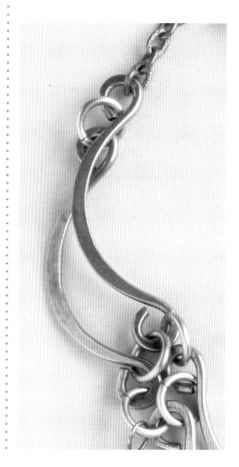

6 Flatten all the arches with the hammer and the steel block. Do a bit more hammering at the center of the arch and at the end loops.

7 Use the round-nose pliers to tighten up the flattened loops so they look completely closed.

8 File away any tool marks at the loop ends.

TEARDROP DANGLES

9 Insert one of the pieces of the 24-gauge wire into a teardrop bead. Shift the wire so that the bead is ¾ inch (2 cm) from one end. Cross the ends.

10 Using the very tip of the chain-nose pliers, align the longer end of the wire so that it stands up vertically from the end of the bead (figure 2).

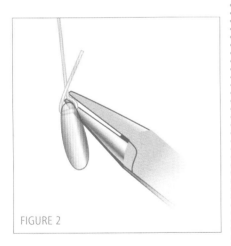

FIGURE 2

11 Grip the two wires with the chain-nose pliers at the top of the bead. Wrap the shorter wire end as tightly and as closely to the bead as possible (figure 3).

FIGURE 3

12 Cut the excess from the short wire. Use the flat-nose pliers to compress the end in against the longer wire. File the cut end smooth.

13 Grasp the remaining wire at the marked position on the round-nose pliers and form a loop (figure 4). Use the chain-nose pliers to align the loop with the top of the teardrop bead. Hold the loop in the flat-nose pliers so you can wrap the top of the teardrop with a wire cap (figure 5). Extend the cap enough to cover the drilled hole. Continue the wrapping back up to just below the loop.

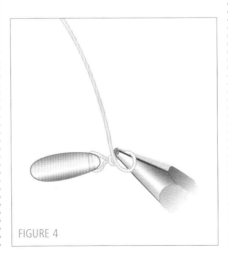

FIGURE 4

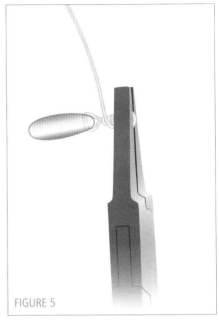

FIGURE 5

14 Cut off any excess wire. Use the chain-nose pliers to snap the cut end to the loop. File smooth the end of the wire if needed.

15 Repeat the wire-cap wrapping (steps 9–14) for the other two beads.

COMPONENTS

16 On an open jump ring, add a longer U-shaped wire, a wrapped teardrop bead, and a longer U-shaped wire, then close the ring. Join the other beads to the remaining longer curved wires in the same way, making sure the beads are all on the same side of the wires. This is the lower component.

17 Join the four shorter curved wires by their loops with three jump rings. This is the upper component.

18 Align the top and bottom components. Starting at one end, join each pair of loops with a jump ring.

CLASP

19 For the hook end of the clasp, cut a 2½-inch (6.3 cm) piece from the 5½-inch (14 cm) 16-gauge wire. Holding the tip of the wire in the jaws of the chain-nose pliers, smoothly file its sharp end with the needle file. Repeat the filing at the other end, too.

20 Grasp the wire with the very tip of the round-nose pliers and form a small loop.

21 Using the 10-mm barrel on the stepped pliers, grasp the wire as close as possible to the loop (figure 6). Turn the wire into a full loop.

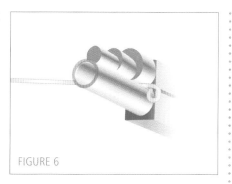

FIGURE 6

22 Use the round-nose pliers to make a slightly larger loop at the other end of the wire.

23 Snip the last of the 16-gauge wire so that it's 1⅜ inches (3.5 cm) long. Fashion it into a figure eight–shaped link, using the jaw of the round-nose pliers as a mandrel. Make sure the figure eight's loops are big enough so that the smaller end of the clasp's hook can pass through.

24 Hammer flat both the hook and the link, then tighten up all of the loops' ends and file smooth all of the tool marks.

25 Attach the chain to the clasp's hook. Open a jump ring and connect one end of the chain to an end loop on the upper component. Use the flat-nose pliers to open one of the hook's loops. Insert a chain link into the open loop, then close it.

26 Attach the other chain section to the other end of the necklace component and to the figure-eight link.

27 Polish the necklace for at least one hour in the tumbler with stainless steel shot mix and a bit of dishwashing liquid. Rinse the necklace and let it air-dry.

28 Oxidize the necklace with a commercial darkening solution that gives the metal a brown patina. Buff the metal with the jewelry polishing cloth.

MATERIALS

6 moss green faceted Picasso-finish glass beads, 6 x 3 mm

2 peach-colored aventurine flower beads, 8 mm

2 pieces of copper wire, 20 gauge, each 3 inches (7.6 cm) long*

6 non-tarnish copper head pins, each 4 inches (10.2 cm) long

1 pair of non-tarnish copper ear wires

* If 20 gauge isn't available, use 22 instead.

TOOLS

Round-nose pliers

Needle-nose pliers

Flush wire cutters

DIMENSIONS

Length, 1⅝ inches (4.1 cm)

Designed by **REBECCA SANCHEZ**

This design pairs peachy carved flower beads with melon-colored dangles. Tasty!

Peach Aventurine Earrings

INSTRUCTIONS

1 String one of the green beads onto one of the head pins.

2 Use the round-nose pliers to make a 90° bend in the wire just above the bead. Use the needle-nose pliers to bring the tail around one jaw of the round-nose pliers. Make several wraps (figure 1).

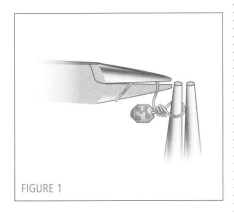

FIGURE 1

3 Trim the wrap closely with the cutters. Use the needle-nose pliers to tuck the end against the wrap.

4 Repeat steps 1–3 to create wrapped loops on the remaining five 6 x 3-mm beads.

5 Use the round-nose pliers to grasp the 20-gauge wire ½ inch (1.3 cm) from one end. Turn the wire to make a 90° bend there. Form a loop in the longer tail, just beyond the bend (figure 2).

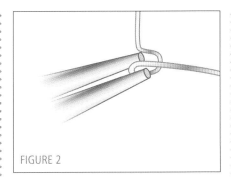

FIGURE 2

6 Use the needle-nose pliers to twist the loop open a bit. String three of your wrapped loop beads onto the loop made in step 5.

7 Grasp the loop with the round-nose pliers. Use the needle-nose pliers to wrap the loop with the shorter tail wire (figure 3). Trim the wire and tuck it in if necessary.

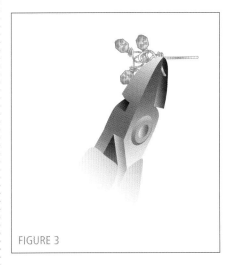

FIGURE 3

8 String one of the 8-mm flowers onto the longer tail.

9 Create a wrapped loop at the top of the flower bead, as you did in steps 2 and 3.

10 Use the needle-nose pliers to twist open one of the ear wires' loops. Add the earring, then twist the loop back in place.

11 Repeat steps 5–10 to complete your second earring.

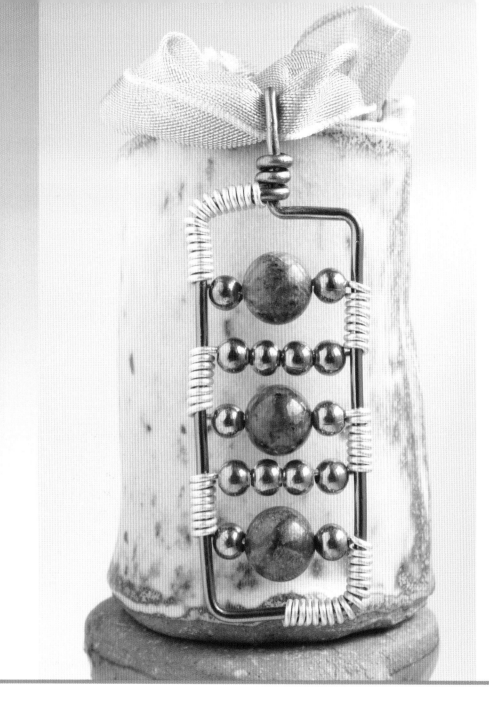

MATERIALS

14 copper round beads, 4 mm

3 unakite round beads, 8 mm

9 inches (22.9 cm) of antique brass–finish aluminum wire, 16 gauge

25 inches (63.5 cm) of silver-finish aluminum wire, 22 gauge

TOOLS

Wire-straightening pliers

Nylon-tipped flat-nose pliers

Round-nose pliers

Tape measure

Felt-tip marker

Flush wire cutters

Needle file

DIMENSIONS

⅞ x 2⅜ inches (2.2 x 6 cm)

Designed by **JERRIE ANDERSON**

Unakite Copper Pendant

The beauty of pink-and-green unakite is married with bright copper beads in this abacus-inspired pendant.

INSTRUCTIONS

1 Use masking tape or another nonslip surface to arrange your beads so they match the layout shown in the sample. Measure the outside width and length of the group as a whole (figure 1). My layout measured ¾ x 1½ inches (1.9 x 3.8 cm).

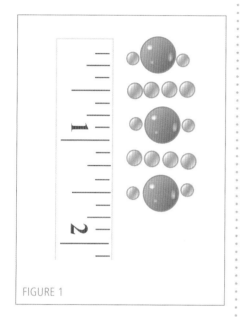

FIGURE 1

2 Straighten the brass-finish wire with wire-straightening pliers. Use a felt-tip marker to make marks at 2¼ inches (5.7 cm), 4 inches (10.2 cm), 4¾ inches (12.1 cm), and 6½ inches (16.5 cm) from one end of the wire.

3 Position the flat-nose pliers just past the 4-inch (10.2 cm) mark and bend the wire up next to the pliers. Move the pliers to just inside the 4¾-inch (12.1 cm) mark and bend the wire up again, to form a U shape. Using the same method, bend the wire again at the first and last marks so that the wire is shaped into a rectangle. The tails from the first and last bends should cross each other (figure 2).

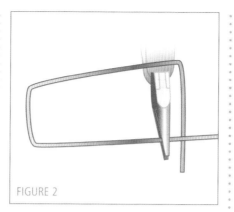

FIGURE 2

4 Mark a point that's halfway across the width (not the length) at the open end of the frame and bend one of the wires up to form a 90° angle (figure 3).

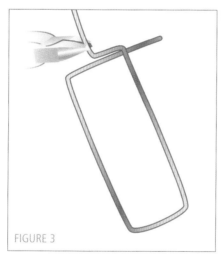

FIGURE 3

5 You'll use the 25-inch (63.5 cm) piece of the silver-finish, 22-gauge wire to make the wraps and secure the beads to the frame. Starting on the frame just to the left of the straight wire section you made in step 4, wind the wire around the frame. For greater control as you wrap, leave yourself a 1-inch (2.5 cm) tail to hold on to. After you've turned the first corner, wrap the frame seven more times and stop when the wire is at the back of the frame (figure 4).

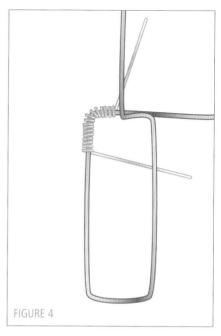

FIGURE 4

6 String one copper bead, one unakite bead, and another copper bead onto the wire. Lap the tail over the opposite frame (figure 5). Wrap the wire around this side of the frame eight times, stopping with the wire at the back of the frame.

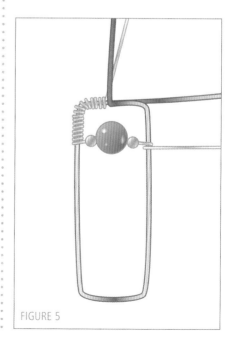

FIGURE 5

Unakite Copper Pendant

7 String four copper beads onto the tail and continue wrapping in the pattern established in step 6 (figure 6), until you've used all of your beads. After you have finished your eighth wrap on the last row of beads, pause and adjust all of the rows and wraps, so that they are equally spaced, by sliding the wrapped wire gently along the frame. Be sure the last row's wraps sit snugly along the bottom of the frame before you continue the wrapping around the bottom corner and halfway across the shorter side of the frame.

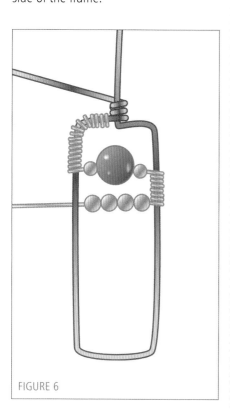

FIGURE 6

8 Trim the wrapping wire's tail with the flush wire cutters. Use the flat-nose pliers to tightly wrap the cut end to the frame. Trim the starting wrap at the top of the frame, and repeat this tightening process.

9 Carefully wrap the straight frame tail of the 16-gauge wire around the bent tail three times (figure 7). Trim the wrapped wire, using the flush wire cutters, on the back side of the frame.

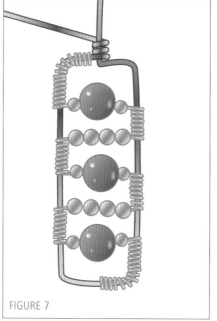

FIGURE 7

10 Using round-nose pliers, wrap the bent wire to the back of the frame to make the bail. Trim it close to the frame (figure 8). Run your finger along the piece to check the ends of the wires. Gently file any sharp edges.

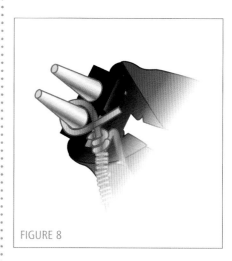

FIGURE 8

Designed by **NATHALIE MORNU**

Celadon & Steel Bangles

There's really no wrong way to make these stylish bangles.

MATERIALS

1 spool of dark annealed 19-gauge steel wire

2 yards (1.8 m) of dark annealed 28-gauge steel wire

13 pale blue top-drilled glass drops, 10 mm

3 smoky glass drops, 10 mm

TOOLS

Wire cutters

Flat-nose pliers

DIMENSIONS

Diameter, 2⅝ inches (6.7 cm)

Celadon & Steel Bangles

INSTRUCTIONS

1 Without changing its curvature, gently unspool enough of the 19-gauge wire to go three times around your wrist loosely. This is the armature that you'll build upon.

2 Cut 1 yard (91.4 cm) of 19-gauge wire. Before you can wrap it around a section of the armature, you'll need to secure it. This is the tricky part. Use your pliers to shape a tiny hook at one end of the wire and then hold it clamped to a spot on the armature.

3 Wrap the wire tightly around the armature a few times until eventually it stays in place without your having to keep it clamped with the pliers. At this point, you can experiment with different ways of wrapping your way around the armature:

- tight or loose
- sparse or thick
- messy or orderly
- several times in the same spot to form a clump
- over and over in the same spot until you've got a big knot.

When you run out of wire, tuck the end securely into some nearby wraps to hide it. Then cut a new piece of wire, make a wee hook in one end, secure it into the existing wraps with the help of the pliers, and keep wrapping your way around the armature.

4 After wrapping all of the armature in wire, trim off any extra wire, then hide the end by tucking it securely into some nearby wraps.

5 Use short pieces of the 28-gauge wire to attach the glass drops here and there on the bangle, tucking each bead inside a clump of existing wire-wrapping to help hold it snugly.

6 Repeat all steps to make two more bangles.

MATERIALS

2 red heart-shaped crystal briolettes, 12 mm

2 pieces of oxidized brass wire, 24 gauge, each 9 inches (22.9 cm) long

2 pieces of oxidized brass wire, 20 gauge, each 2¼ inches (5.7 cm) long

TOOLS

Chain-nose pliers

Round-nose pliers

Flush wire cutters

Permanent marker

Wooden dowels, ⁵⁄₁₆ inch (8 mm) and ³⁄₈ inch (1 cm) in diameter

Ball-peen hammer and steel block

Jeweler's file

Steel wool, grade 0000

Tweezers

Pretreated polishing pad

DIMENSIONS

Length, 1⁵⁄₁₆ inches (3.3 cm)

Designed by **KAMMY PIETRASZEK**

Red Magma Earrings

These BNO (Big Night Out) earrings are made with deep-strawberry crystal hearts, hugged by brass and dangled from elongated ear wires.

Red Magma Earrings

INSTRUCTIONS

DANGLES

1 String a heart-shaped bead to the middle of one of the 24-gauge pieces of wire. Cross the tails over the top of the bead as tightly as possible.

2 Bring one of the wire tails over the top of the bead and thread it back through the hole a second time (figure 1). Pull the wire so it's wrapped snugly through the hole.

FIGURE 1

3 Using the chain-nose pliers, bring the wire back to a center point on top of the bead. Again, cross both wire tails over the top of the bead so that they are tight. The pair of wires should be standing straight up, over the center of the bead.

4 Grasping the two wires together with the round-nose pliers, make a simple loop.

5 Wrap the paired wires three times, from the base of the loop you just made down to the top of the heart. Wrap them back up and over the first wraps four or five times more, or until the wire is used.

6 Snip the ends of the wires with the wire cutters, and press their ends firmly into the back of the wire bundle with the chain-nose pliers.

7 Repeat steps 1–6 to make a second dangle.

EAR WIRES

8 Use the marker to mark a jaw of the round-nose pliers 2 mm from the tip.

9 Set the end of one of the 20-gauge wires onto the mark on the round-nose pliers. Use the pliers to create a simple "dangle loop" in the wire. Turn the end of the other wire in the same way.

10 Make a mark on one of the wires that is ¾ inch (1.9 cm) away from the loop end. With their loops together, bend both ear wires over the ⁵⁄₁₆-inch (8 mm) dowel to create a large earlobe curve. Shape them as shown in figure 2.

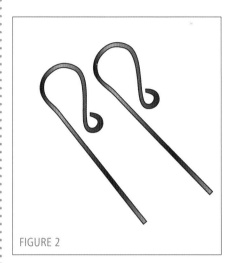

FIGURE 2

11 Flatten the ear wire curves with the ball-peen hammer on the steel block. Use the chain-nose pliers to squeeze the dangle loop closed again (it will open slightly from the hammering).

12 Slide the curved wires onto the ³⁄₈-inch (1 cm) dowel. (Reshape if necessary to make sure the ear wires still match.) Use the ⁵⁄₁₆-inch (8 mm) dowel to bring just the ends of the ear wires up from under the dowel, as shown in figure 3. Keep the wires on both dowels while you trim their ends to the desired length with the flush wire cutters. Remove the ear wires from the dowels.

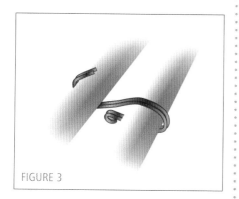

FIGURE 3

13 Smooth the ends of the ear wires with the jeweler's file, then lightly hammer them, using the ball-peen hammer on the block.

14 Use the chain-nose pliers to open a dangle loop of the ear wires as you would a jump ring. Catch one of the bead links in the opened dangle loop. Close the loop with the chain-nose pliers the same way you opened it. Add the other bead link to the other ear wire.

FINAL FINISH

15 Rubbing in one direction only, polish the brass wire with the steel wool. Use the tweezers to pick out any stray pieces of steel wool that may have caught in the wire.

16 Use the polishing pad to give the brass its final polish.

MATERIALS

7 green amethyst briolettes,
8–12 mm, in graduated pairs

1 green amethyst briolette, 14 mm

3 inches (7.6 cm) of half-hard 14k
gold–filled wire, 16 gauge

36 inches (91.4 cm) of dead-soft 14k
gold–filled wire, 26 gauge

4½ inches (11.4 cm) of half-hard 14k
gold–filled wire, 18 gauge

14 inches (35.6 cm) of round gold-
filled belcher-style chain, 2 mm

TOOLS

Round-nose pliers

Flat-nose pliers

Large wooden dowel, similar in
diameter to a wooden broom
handle

Hammer and steel block

Flush wire cutters

Jeweler's file

DIMENSIONS

Length, 17¹⁵⁄₁₆ inches (45.6 cm)

Designed by BONNIE RICONDA

Make this dressy piece—an array of graduated green amethyst briolettes—with a handful of tools and a few simple techniques.

Green Amethyst Necklace

INSTRUCTIONS

1 Gently curve the piece of 16-gauge wire against the dowel. Use the round-nose pliers to make a partial loop at each end of the wire. Turn the loops in the direction opposite the wire's overall curve. This is the frame that will hold the stones.

2 Use the hammer and the steel block to flatten the frame. Don't flatten the loops yet.

3 Fold the chain in half and hold it away from your body with the fold hanging down. Cut the very bottommost link in the fold. Slip the last link of one chain piece into one of the frame's loops. Squeeze this loop closed with the flat-nose pliers. Do the same for the other loop. Flatten both of the loops. Avoid hammering the chain, because that could break a link.

4 Starting next to the frame's left-hand loop, wrap the center of the 26-gauge wire several times around it. Tighten the wraps against the frame with the flat-nose pliers.

5 Slide one of the smallest stones onto the center of the 26-gauge wire. Hold the drilled end of the stone in place,

right next to one of the frame loops, with your thumb. Wrap the left-hand tail wire (the tail nearest the loop) neatly and tightly three or four times around the frame and also around the drilled end of the stone. This will leave a long tail wire to the left of the stone.

6 Now, you'll add the rest of the stones to the frame, from left to right, working with the right-hand tail. Wrap the frame a few times with the right-hand tail. Thread a larger briolette onto the right-hand tail. Holding that stone in place, wrap the top of the stone, and then the frame again.

7 Repeat the wrapping until you have wrapped all of the stones onto the frame with the largest stone in the center and tapering in size to the smallest stone. Secure the end of the right-hand tail wire, then cut any excess. Use the flat-nose pliers to securely compress this cut end of the wire into the wrapped frame.

8 Crisscross the left-hand tail wire all across the frame, then repeat the same process back in the other direction. When the wrapping again reaches the left-hand end of the frame, cut any excess wire. Compress the cut end against the frame with the flat-nose pliers.

9 For the clasp's eye, cut the 18-gauge wire into a 2¾-inch (7 cm) piece and a 1¾-inch (4.4 cm) piece. Make a loop in one end of the longer piece with the round-nose pliers. Shape the loop into a spiral. Shape the rest of the wire into a figure eight by using the pliers like a mandrel (figures 1 and 2).

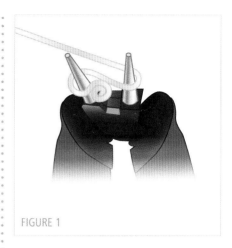

FIGURE 1

FIGURE 2

10 Where the wire completes the figure eight, bend the tail at a 90° angle, as shown in figure 3. Cut the tail ¾ inch (1.9 cm) away from the figure eight, as shown in figure 3.

FIGURE 3

11 Flatten and texture the figure eight, but not the ¾-inch (1.9 cm) tail, with the hammer and the bench block. Feed the end of a chain piece onto the tail and into the figure eight. Finish the flattening and texturing, being careful not to hit any of the chain's links.

12 For the clasp's hook, make a spiral at one end of the 1¾-inch (4.4 cm) piece you cut in step 9, using the flat-nose pliers to tightly curl it. Bend the wire into a hook shape by wrapping it around the round-nose pliers, as shown in figure 3.

13 Bend the tail of the hook a little bit, then cut it to your desired length. File the tip of the cut end with the jeweler's file. Use the hammer and bench block to flatten and texture the hook, except for the bent end.

14 Feed an end link of chain onto the hook clasp and position it next to the loop. Use the flat-nose pliers to close the loop spiral (figure 4). Finish the flattening and texturing at the hook's open end. Avoid hitting the chain's links.

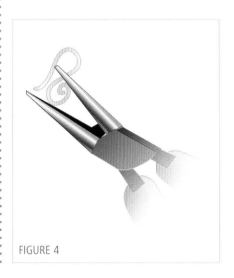

FIGURE 4

MATERIALS

2 silver disk beads

2 bird-shaped glass beads

2 silver round beads, 1 mm

12 inches (30.5 cm) of 18-gauge silver wire

2 inches (5.1 cm) of silver chain

6 jump rings, 4 mm

1 pair of silver ear wires

2 silver head pins

TOOLS

Round-nose pliers

Flush wire cutters

2 pairs of flat-nosed pliers

Permanent marker

DIMENSIONS

Length, $2\frac{7}{8}$ inches (7.3 cm)

Designed by NATHALIE MORNU

Novelty beads become even more fun when they're captured in silver frames.

Cardinal Rules Earrings

Cardinal Rules Earrings

INSTRUCTIONS

1 Cut the wire in half. Set one piece aside.

2 To start making the large oval element, make a mark ⁵⁄₁₆ inch (8 mm) from each end of the wire. At each mark, use the round-nose pliers to make a 90° bend in the wire. Form each of the short bent tails into a loop with round-nose pliers.

3 Using the piece of wire set aside in step 1, repeat step 2.

4 Form both pieces of wire into an oval shape, as shown in figure 1. Holding each element the way it will hang from your lobe, twist each of the four loops at the ends of the wires so they're parallel to the floor.

5 Cut the piece of chain in half. Set one piece aside.

6 Open a jump ring. Working with either of the oval elements, catch one loop in the jump ring, then one end of the chain, then the other loop. Close the jump ring. Repeat to make a second, identical element.

7 Now you'll attach the ear wires. Open a jump ring. Catch an ear wire in it, then the jump ring holding together the ends of an oval element. Close the jump ring. Repeat to attach the remaining ear wire to the other oval element.

8 Finally, attach the bird-shaped beads as follows: slide a silver disk bead, a bird bead, and a silver round onto a head pin. Finish the head pin with a loop close to the beads, and cut off any extra wire. Use a jump ring to attach this dangle to the free end of the chain in one of the elements. *Note*: You may have to shorten the chain. Repeat to finish the other earring.

FIGURE 1

Designed by BONNIE RICONDA

A veritable riot of briolette gems in deep and fruity colors pairs up with plenty of gold wire in this double-hoop design.

Double
Jewel Hoops

MATERIALS

34 amethyst, topaz, tanzanite, and peridot round and oval briolettes in graduated sizes, 3–10 mm

2 peridot teardrop briolettes, 12 mm

2 pieces of 14 karat gold–filled wire, 18 gauge, each 9 inches (22.9 cm) long

36 inches (91.4 cm) of 14 karat gold–filled wire, 26 gauge

2 pieces of 14 karat gold–filled wire, 20 gauge, each 2 inches (5.1 cm) long

TOOLS

Round-nose pliers

Flat-nose pliers with nylon-coated jaws

Mandrels, 1⅝ inches (4.1 cm), 1 inch (2.5 cm), and ¼ inch (6 mm) in diameter

Flush wire cutters

Hammer and steel block

Needle file

DIMENSIONS

Length, 2¹⁄₁₆ inches (5.2 cm)

Double Jewel Hoops

INSTRUCTIONS

1 Curl one end of a 9-inch (22.9 cm) piece of 18-gauge wire with the tip of the round-nose pliers. Make another curl at the end of the other piece of 18-gauge wire.

2 Holding the uncurled ends together, shape the paired wires around a mandrel so they form outer hoops that measure 1⅝ inches (4 cm) in diameter (figure 1). Any firm, round object, such as a plastic bottle cap, can be a mandrel.

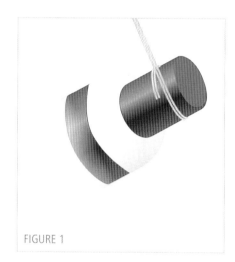

FIGURE 1

3 Switching to a smaller mandrel, shape the rest of the wire into inner hoops that are 1 inch (2.5 cm) in diameter. The hoops will still have an open, spiral-like shape at this point. Curl the remaining two wire ends as you did in step 2 (figure 2).

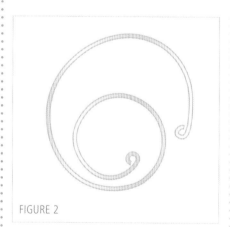

FIGURE 2

4 Flush-cut the very tips of the curls you made in step 1. Compare the two hoops to make sure they are the same size.

5 Add some light texture to the hoops, using the hammer and the steel block.

6 Make two groups of 11 mixed gemstones, graduating them in size and shape so they look like the arrangement on the outer hoops shown in the sample, with a large teardrop briolette at each center. Arrange the rest of the stones into two groups of seven stones each for the inner hoops.

7 Starting at the 9 o'clock position on one of the outer hoops, wrap the fine 26-gauge wire several times around the hoop wire. Starting with the smallest one, string a group of eleven stones, one by one, onto the 26-gauge wire.

8 Move the first stone into place on the outer hoop. Wrap the wire around the end of the stone, then around the hoop wire several times. Move each of the stones into place this way, using more wraps for the larger stones (so they stay stable), until you've added 11 stones. The wrapping should end at the 3 o'clock point on the larger hoop.

9 Cut any excess wire. Use the flat-nose pliers to crimp the 26-gauge wire you wrapped around the outer hoop. Repeat steps 7–9 for the other outer hoop.

10 Wrap your stones onto the inner hoops as you did for the outer ones.

11 With the very tip of the round-nose pliers, make a tiny curl at one end of a piece of the 20-gauge wire. Do the same for the other piece.

12 Shifting the wire into the pliers' jaws as you go, shape the rest of the wire into an S curve, as shown in figure 3. Do the same for the other 2-inch (5.1 cm) piece. To check their size and shape, lay them down on figure 3.

Actual Size

FIGURE 3

13 With the tip of a pen (or other small dowel) that is ¼ inch (6 mm) in diameter, curl the tips of the ear wires. Line up the two curved ear wire pieces with each other and make sure they match. File the cut ends of the wires. Lightly texture the

smaller (front-facing) sections of the ear wires with the hammer.

14 Align the curled ends of a hoop one over the other. Lay them down on figure 4 so they mimic the shape and size as shown. Slip them both over the tail of the ear wire, slide them into the front loop, and then close the ear wire's loop with your round-nose pliers. Add the ear wire to the other hoop in the same way.

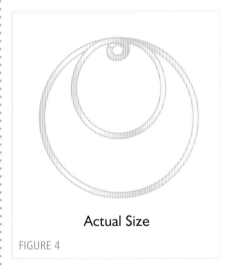

Actual Size

FIGURE 4

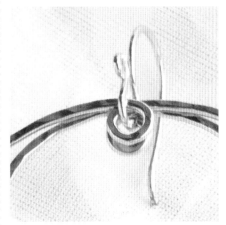

Asymmetrical Amethyst Necklace

If you're not all about matchy-matchy style, this piece plays right into your asymmetrical aesthetic.

Designed by ELISABETH ALLERTON

MATERIALS

1 pink amethyst rondelle, 4 mm

3 medium-purple amethyst rondelles, 3 mm

2 dark purple (royal) amethyst rondelles, 3 mm

1 amethyst briolette, 12 x 15 mm

6½ inches (16.5 cm) of sterling silver wire, 20 gauge

56 inches (1.4 m) of sterling silver wire, 28 gauge

14 inches (35.6 cm) of sterling silver 2-mm curb chain

1¼ inches (3.2 cm) of extender chain

1 sterling silver lobster clasp, 6 mm, with attached jump ring

1 sterling silver head pin, 28 gauge

TOOLS

Round-nose pliers

Flush wire cutters

Steel mandrel, 12 mm

Liver of sulfur

Steel wool, grade 0000

Soft toothbrush

DIMENSIONS

Chain length, 17½ inches (44.5 cm)

Focal length, 2⅜ inches (6 cm)

INSTRUCTIONS

1 Working at one end of the 20-gauge wire, form a large teardrop-shaped wrapped loop over the mandrel, but don't trim the wrapping wire yet. There should be enough of the tail wire left to make another, smaller loop. Use the round-nose pliers to shape this tail into a much smaller wrapped loop. Make this bail big enough so that your chain can pass through it. Close this new loop by wrapping it in the direction opposite that used for the larger teardrop loop. Now cut the ends of the two wires so they meet neatly on the wrap (figure 1).

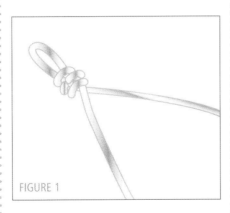

FIGURE 1

2 Tightly wrap the teardrop (but not the wrapped loop at the top) with a 14-inch (35.6 cm) piece of 28-gauge wire. Cut any excess wire and tuck the wire's end to the inside of the frame.

3 Use a 16-inch (40.6 cm) piece of 28-gauge wire to lash three rondelles to one side of the teardrop frame, with the largest one at the bottom:

- a 4-mm pink
- a medium-purple 3-mm
- a dark purple 3-mm

When they're securely attached to the frame, bring your working wire to one end of the group of rondelles. You'll still have a long tail of wire (figure 2). Wrap this tail with a 12-inch (30 cm) piece of 28-gauge wire, then weave this wrapped-wire portion in and around the rondelles. Be sure to bring the last of the wire to one end of the group of rondelles so you can securely tuck the end of it in.

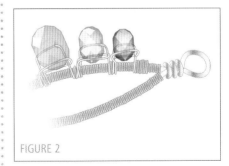

FIGURE 2

4 Now it's time to attach the focal bead—the briolette—to the frame. Pull a 12-inch (30.5 cm) piece of 28-gauge wire through the briolette. Leave a

Asymmetrical Amethyst Necklace

2-inch (5.1 cm) tail on one side, with the rest coming out the other side. Pinch the wire's ends so they cross each other. Wrap the longer piece around and around the shorter piece until the wrapping measures ¾ inch (1.9 cm) long.

5 Curve the wrapped section around the jaw of the round-nose pliers to create a bail (figure 3). Slide the bail through the frame.

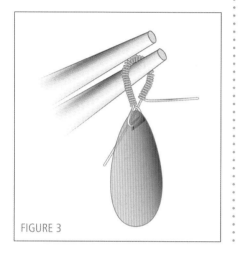

FIGURE 3

6 Form a wire cap around the top of the briolette by first wrapping it with the shorter tail and then the longer one. Trim the excess and tuck in the ends.

7 Slip your chain through the frame's top loop. Attach the clasp to one end of the chain with the jump ring that came with it.

8 Make a loop at one end of a 2-inch (5.1 cm) section of 28-gauge wire. Slip it onto the other end of the chain. Wrap the loop a few times, then trim the short end of the wire. Slide two 3-mm rondelles, one medium and one dark, onto the wire (figure 4). Make another loop through one end of a five-link piece of extender chain. Wrap the loop and trim away any excess wire. Using the head pin, wrap a medium-purple amethyst rondelle to the other end of the extender chain.

FIGURE 4

9 Oxidize the whole piece with liver of sulfur. Once it's as dark as you like, rinse the piece thoroughly. Polish the piece with the ultra-fine steel wool. If pieces of steel wool remain in the jewelry, scrub them *gently* away with the toothbrush.

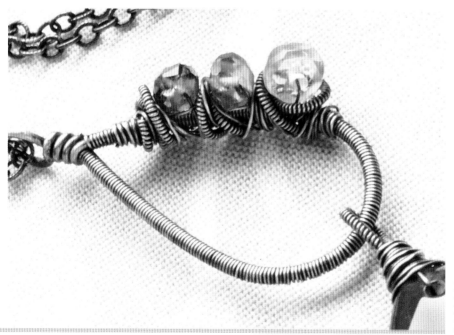

MATERIALS

7 round blue sponge coral beads, 14 mm

7 pieces of uncoated round copper wire, 20 gauge, each 9 inches (22.9 cm) long

7 pieces of uncoated round copper wire, 26 gauge, each 24 inches (61 cm) long

2 pieces of uncoated copper curb-link chain, each 3½ inches (8.9 cm) long

3½ inches (8.9 cm) of 14-gauge copper wire

12 uncoated copper jump rings, 18 gauge, 6 mm

2 uncoated copper jump rings, 16 gauge, 7 mm

2 uncoated copper jump rings, 16 gauge, 8 mm

TOOLS

Round-nose pliers

Bent-nose pliers

Nylon wire-straightening pliers (optional)

2 pairs of flat-nose pliers

Flush wire cutters

Chasing hammer and bench block

Wire-wrapping mandrel, 9 mm diameter

Liver of sulfur

Steel wool, grade 0000

Wire brush (optional)

Jewelry tumbler and stainless steel shot (optional)

DIMENSIONS

Length, 20¾ inches (52.7 cm)

Designed by **BRENDA DAVIS**

Blue Coral Necklace

The coppery gleam of herringbone weave complements dramatically oversized blue sponge coral beads in this simple stunner.

Blue Coral Necklace

INSTRUCTIONS

1 Using round-nose pliers, make a wrapped loop 3 inches (7.6 cm) from the end of a piece of 9-inch (22.9 cm) 20-gauge wire. Wrap the wire tightly nine times to make a ³/₈-inch (1 cm) shank. Trim with flush wire cutters and tuck in the wire end with the bent-nose pliers.

2 Slide a bead onto the wire until it's flush against the shank. Make a wrapped loop ³/₈ inch (1 cm) from the bead, then wrap that shank tightly eight times (figure 1), leaving a gap. Trim the excess wire and tuck in the end with bent-nose pliers.

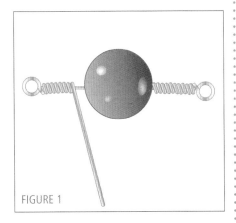

FIGURE 1

3 Attach one of the 24-inch (60.1 cm) pieces of 26-gauge wire to the shank with the gap in it by wrapping it four or five times. Trim and tuck in this small piece of wire. If necessary, use the nylon pliers to straighten the remaining length of the wire.

4 To begin the weave, hold the bead sideways. Bring the long wire across the bead and around to the bottom of the other shank end. Wrap the wire around this wrapped shank once, as shown in figure 2. Repeat this wrap to bring the wire back to the starting shank and wrap it there. This is the foundation for the herringbone weave.

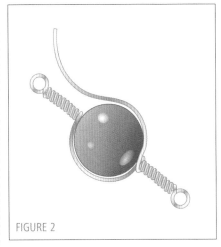

FIGURE 2

Continue wrapping until you have seven wires on each side of the bead. Trim and tuck any excess wire with your bent-nose pliers. You now have one woven bead set (figure 3).

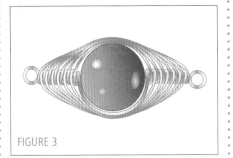

FIGURE 3

5 Repeat steps 1–4 for the remaining six beads.

6 Join all of the woven bead sets with pairs of 6-mm jump rings.

7 Use a 7-mm jump ring to connect a piece of curb-link chain to each end of the connected bead sets.

8 Attach an 8-mm jump ring to each end of the copper curb-link chain.

9 Make the clasp from the piece of 14-gauge copper wire. First, flatten the tips of this wire with the chasing hammer on the bench block. Now create a small loop at each end with the tips of the round-nose pliers; the loops should curl in opposite directions.

10 Shape one end of the wire over the 9-mm wire-wrapping mandrel. Shape another curve at the other end in the opposite direction (figure 4). Use the chasing hammer on the bench block to flatten the large curves of the clasp. Texture the curves with the ball-peen end of the chasing hammer.

FIGURE 4

11 Attach the S-clasp to each of the 8-mm copper jump rings on the ends of the curb-link chain. Add a liver of sulfur patina. Use the steel wool to buff the wire and remove excess patina. Get a higher shine with a brass wire brush. Tumble the piece in a tumbler with stainless steel shot for 15 to 20 minutes to shine up and harden the copper.

MATERIALS

2 lilac cat's-eye star beads, 6 mm

2 pieces of light purple non-tarnish, silver-plated copper wire, 22 gauge, each 10 inches (25.4 cm) long

2 pieces of dark purple non-tarnish, silver-plated copper wire, 22 gauge, each 10 inches (25.4 cm) long

1 pair of purple anodized niobium loop ear wires

TOOLS

Round-nose pliers

2 pairs of chain-nose pliers with nylon-coated jaws*

Flush wire cutters

Chasing hammer and steel bench block

* I treated my pliers with a rubberlike coating to keep tool marks off the wire. If you use the product, take care to follow the manufacturer's instructions.

DIMENSIONS

Length, 2⁷⁄₁₆ inches (6.2 cm)

Designed by KENDRA TORNHEIM

Trace the path of a shooting star in the night sky with swirls of purple craft wire.

Star Swirl Earrings

INSTRUCTIONS

DANGLE LOOP

1 Hold together one piece of the light purple wire and one piece of the dark purple wire. Place the midpoint of the wires well back into the jaws of the round-nose pliers, with the dark purple wire lying closer to the pliers' opening. Bend the paired wires in half over one jaw of the pliers. This is the first set of wires.

2 Cross the farther pair of wires toward you over the other two ends. Twist both pairs of wires two full turns toward yourself.

3 Repeat step 1 with the other two wires.

4 Repeat step 2, but mirror the actions: cross the pair that is closer to you away from yourself. Twist the pairs two full turns away from yourself. You've made the second set of wires.

EARRING BODY

5 Work with the first set of wires you made in steps 1 and 2. The left-hand pair of wires emerges from the back of the twist. Curve the left wires up, around into a clockwise partial circle, then back to the left, as shown in figure 1.

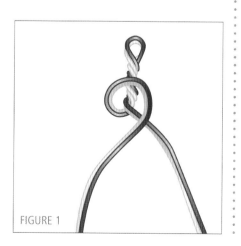

FIGURE 1

6 Curve the light purple wire from the right pair across the left pair. Slide a star bead onto this wire. Position it as shown in figure 2.

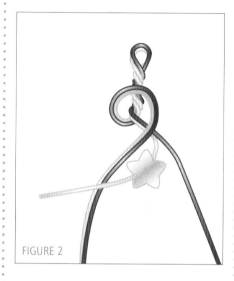

FIGURE 2

7 Make three wraps around the left-hand pair of wires with the tail that has the star on it. Use the cutters to trim it at the back of the earring.

8 Make a loop underneath the star with the pair of wires (figure 3).

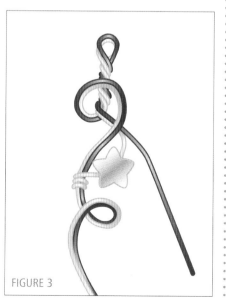

FIGURE 3

9 Use the bare single wire to make a loop on the back of the earring, directly behind the star. Curve the end of the wire down and cross it in front of the pair of wires (figure 4).

FIGURE 4

10 Space apart the two loops by making the inner loop a little smaller (pull the dark purple wire slightly tighter). Feed a little of the light purple wire back to make the outer loop slightly larger.

11 Wrap the single dark purple wire, from right to left, twice around the paired wires. Use the chain-nose pliers to compress the wrap tightly.

Star Swirl Earrings

12 Spread the three tails apart. Use the cutters to trim each wire to a 1-inch (2.5 cm) tail (figure 5).

FIGURE 5

13 Make an open spiral with the side wires. Make an open spiral with the center wire, curling it to the left.

14 Gently hammer the spirals on the steel block to texture and harden the wire.

15 Make the second earring body by reversing the left and right directions so that it will be a mirror image of the first one.

FINISH
16 Add an ear wire to each earring body, opening and closing the loop with two pairs of pliers as you would a jump ring.

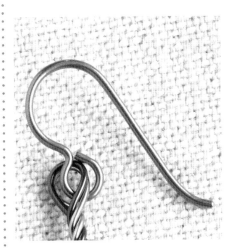

Black Pearls Chain

Create a delicate chain from an intriguing and artful mix of spiral variations and black button pearls, joined by figaro-style chain.

Designed by **COLLEEN GILGENBACH**

MATERIALS

9 black iris cultured button pearls, 8 mm

44¾ inches (1.4 m) of half-hard sterling silver wire, 22 gauge

24 inches (61 cm) of sterling silver figaro-style chain, 4 mm

TOOLS

Round-nose pliers

Chain-nose pliers

Flush wire cutters

Lightweight hammer and steel block

DIMENSIONS

Circumference, 34½ inches (87.6 cm)

Black Pearls Chain

INSTRUCTIONS

Note: Throughout this project you'll work with the entire piece of chain, cutting links only when you need to join a spiral or a wrapped bead loop to it. Just take it slow and enjoy the challenge.

1 Cut the silver wire as follows:

- 2 pieces, 1 inch (2.5 cm) each, for the Tiny Spirals
- 9 pieces, 2¼ inches (5.7 cm) each, for the Wrapped Pearls
- 2 pieces, 5 inches (12.7 cm) each, for the Double Spirals
- 4 pieces, 2 inches (5.1 cm) each, for the Loose Spirals
- 2 pieces, 2¼ inches (5.7 cm) each, for the Double-Wire Spirals

TINY SPIRAL

2 Use the round-nose pliers' tips to make a loop at the end of a 1-inch (2.5 cm) piece of wire. Hold the loop firmly in a wide part of the chain-nose pliers. Use your fingers to shape the tail into a loose spiral. Leave a tail ¼ inch (6 mm) long.

3 Feed one of the chain's end links into an outer turn of the spiral (figure 1). You may have to open the spiral slightly to get the chain link around to this position.

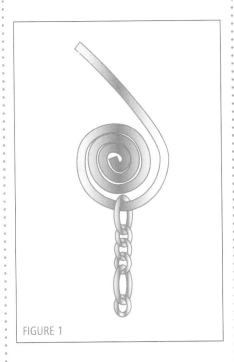

FIGURE 1

4 Start a loop in the spiral's tail, using the tip of the round-nose pliers. Catch the chain's other end link in it, then finish closing the loop.

5 Cut a link in the chain that's 1 inch (2.5 cm) away from the Tiny Spiral you just made.

WRAPPED PEARL

6 Center a 2¼-inch (5.7 cm) piece of wire through a pearl. Start a loop in the wire ⅛ inch (3 mm) away from the pearl. Feed the chain's end link onto the new loop, then wrap that loop closed. Make another loop on the other side of the pearl, catching the chain's other free end in it before you close and wrap it.

7 Cut a link in the chain that's 1 inch (2.5 cm) away from the Wrapped Pearl you just made.

DOUBLE SPIRAL

8 Grasp the center of one of the 5-inch (12.7 cm) pieces of wire with the innermost flat place in the jaws of the chain-nose pliers. Using the pliers as a mandrel, bend one end of the wire up and the other end down, as shown in figure 2. The bent area should be ¼ inch (6 mm) wide. Remove the wire from the pliers.

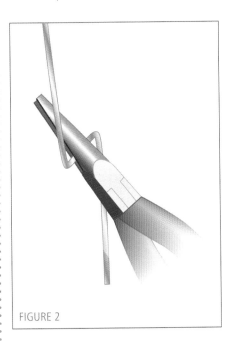

FIGURE 2

9 Feed the open ends of the chain onto the ¼-inch (6 mm) bend in the wire (figure 3).

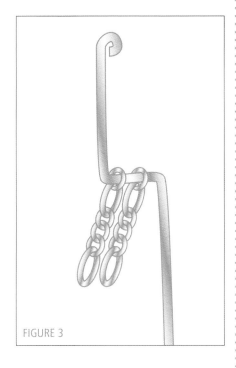

FIGURE 3

10 Form an inward-facing loop at one end of the wire. Hold this loop firmly in the chain-nose pliers. Push the tail around the loop until the outermost turn of the spiral reaches the ¼-inch (6 mm) bend (figure 4). Form a loop at the other end of the wire and make another inward-facing spiral from it. Move the chain's ends into the outermost turns of the two spirals, as shown in figure 5. (You may have to pry them apart slightly to do this.)

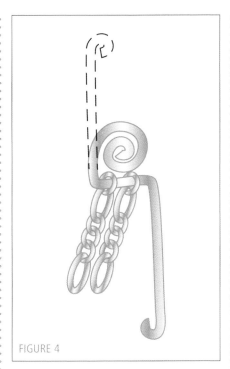

FIGURE 4

FIGURE 5

11 Cut a link in the chain 1 inch (2.5 cm) away from the Double Spiral you just made.

12 Make another Wrapped Pearl and add it to the open ends of the chain.

LOOSE SPIRAL

13 Use the round-nose pliers' tips to make a loop at the end of a 2-inch (5.1 cm) piece of wire. Hold the loop firmly in the flat of the chain-nose pliers. Use your fingers to shape the tail wire into a loosely wound spiral. Leave a straight tail ½ inch (1.3 cm) long.

14 Feed one of the chain's end links into an outer turn of the spiral. You may have to open the spiral slightly to get the chain link around to this position.

15 Start a loop in the spiral's tail, using the tip of the round-nose pliers. Catch the chain's other end link in it, then finish closing the loop.

16 Cut a link in the chain that's 1 inch (2.5 cm) away from the Loose Spiral. Create another Wrapped Pearl and add it to the open ends of the chain.

Black Pearls Chain

DOUBLE-WIRE SPIRAL

17 Fold a 2¼-inch (5.7 cm) piece of the sterling wire in half. Grasp the fold with your round-nose pliers and turn it into a flat loop. Use your chain-nose pliers to form this pair of wires into a single, loose spiral with a 1-inch (2.5 cm) tail. Position the two tail wires so they can be formed into loops on opposite sides of the spiral. Attach the two ends of the chain to the loops before closing them.

18 Cut a link in the chain 1 inch (2.5 cm) away from the Double-Wire Spiral. Create another Wrapped Pearl and add it to the open ends of the chain.

ADD MORE ELEMENTS

19 Continue to add spirals and pearls as follows:

- Loose Spiral
- Wrapped Pearl Loop
- Double Spiral
- Wrapped Pearl Loop
- Loose Spiral
- Wrapped Pearl Loop
- Double-Wire Spiral
- Wrapped Pearl Loop
- Loose Spiral
- Wrapped Pearl Loop
- and one last Tiny Spiral

HAMMERED TEXTURE

20 Use a lightweight hammer on any smooth metal surface to very gently flatten the spirals. Be really careful not to hit the chain.

MATERIALS

18 round aquamarine rondelles, 7 mm*

1 small sterling silver heart charm

6⅜ inches (16 cm) of sterling silver bar-and-link chain

1 round sterling silver toggle clasp, ½ inch (1.3 cm)

3 heavy sterling silver open jump rings, 5 mm

18 sterling silver, 1.5-mm ball-tip head pins, 16 gauge, each 1½ inches (3.8 cm) long*

TOOLS

2 pairs of flat-nose pliers

Round-nose pliers

Bent-nose pliers

Liver of sulfur

Flush wire cutters

Jewelry polishing cloth

* For a finished bracelet 7½ inches (19 cm) long. The number of beads and head pins will change if you make the bracelet a different size.

DIMENSIONS

Length, 7⅜ inches (18.7 cm)

Designed by SHARON CLANCY

Aquamarine & Silver Bracelet

Lit-from-within gemstones really dazzle against the dark patina of a bar-and-link chain.

Aquamarine & Silver Bracelet

INSTRUCTIONS

1 Attach the toggle to one end of the chain with one of the jump rings. Be sure to open and close the jump ring firmly with two pairs of pliers. Move the pliers back and forth several times to harden the metal as you close it. Attach the clasp ring to the other end of the chain in the same way.

2 Apply the liver of sulfur patina to the chain until the silver turns very dark.

3 Put one of the beads onto one of the head pins. Firmly grip your flat-nose pliers ⅛ inch (3 mm) above the stone. Bend the head pin toward you. Grip the bent section of the pin in the jaws of the round-nose pliers, and wrap the wire backward around the top jaw of the pliers. Use the bottom of the pliers to pull the wire toward you and create the loop.

4 Catch the loop that you just created in one of the rings of the chain. Holding the bead in one hand, firmly grip the loop with the flat-nose pliers. Now use the bent-nose pliers to wrap the loop three or four times with the end of the head pin (figure 1).

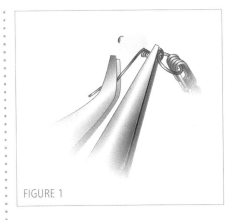

FIGURE 1

5 Repeat steps 3 and 4 to create and attach the wrapped bead loops to each of the links in the chain.

6 Use the flush wire cutters to trim any excess wire from the head pin. Use your bent-nose pliers to pinch down any sharp edges.

7 Attach the charm to the toggle with the remaining 5-mm jump ring, using two pairs of pliers as you did in step 1.

8 Use the polishing cloth to gently buff the silver. Buff it enough to let some of the raised areas of the metal shine through the dark patina. That gives the piece depth and richness.

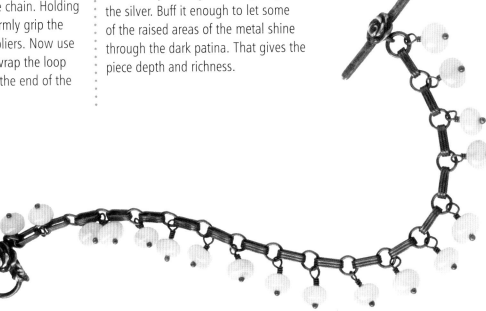

MATERIALS

24 assorted glass and plastic pink-spectrum beads, 4–10 mm*

2 pieces of steel wire, 19 gauge, each 3½ inches (8.9 cm) long

2 pieces of steel wire, 24 gauge, each 3 feet (91.4 cm) long

1 pair of fishhook-style silver-toned ear wires

* Before you start, check to make sure that your wire can pass through all of the beads.

TOOLS

Round-nose pliers

Flush wire cutters

Cloth

Microcrystalline wax

Cotton swab

Jeweler's file

DIMENSIONS

Length, 1¼ inches (3.2 cm)

INSTRUCTIONS

I Use the cloth to clean the carbon off all the pieces of steel wire. Seal the wire pieces with a light coat of microcrystalline wax applied with the cotton swab. File all of the cut ends smooth with the jeweler's file as needed while you work.

Designed by **RICHELLE HAWKS**

A stash-busting design like this pink extravaganza looks pulled together and stylish.

Bead Soup Earrings

Bead Soup Earrings

2 Using the round-nose pliers, make a small loop on one end of the 19-gauge steel wire. Use your hands to form the length of wire into a U shape.

3 String the beads onto the wire, starting with the smallest one. Add beads of increasing size until you reach the approximate midpoint of the wire, and then choose beads of decreasing sizes. Stop when the last bead is ½ inch (1.3 cm) from the end of the wire.

4 Make a loop with the round-nose pliers at the end of the wire (figure 1).

FIGURE 1

5 Twist the loops at both ends laterally for the ear hook attachments.

6 Adjust the hoop so that the loops are ⅝ inch (1.6 cm) apart.

7 Starting 2 inches (5.1 cm) from one end of the 24-gauge wire, wrap the longer end tightly around the middle of the beaded hoop, between two beads. Hold the shorter end of the wire firmly in place until the wrap is secure then leave it alone for now. Use the longer end to do the rest of the wrapping.

8 Wrap the tail up one side of the hoop; cross over each bead tightly and wrap once between each bead.

9 When you reach the loop, wrap the wire around the base tightly two or three times.

10 Work your way back down the line of beads with the wire, crisscrossing them to form a decorative "X" wherever possible. Continue the wrapping all the way to the other loop. When you reach it, wrap the wire around its base two or three times, then continue wrapping back to the starting point using the same crisscrossing technique.

11 When the wrapping is completed, cut the smaller end of the wire to ¾ inch (1.9 cm). Use the jaw of the round-nose pliers to shape it into a tight decorative coil (figure 2).

FIGURE 2

12 Find an appropriate place to feed the longer end of the wire under another piece of the wire to secure, pull firmly,

trim to ¾ inch (2 cm), file smooth, and finish by wrapping and pressing the end or finish with another decorative coil.

13 Repeat steps 1–12 to create the other earring, using the finished earring as a guide to shape and bead placement.

EAR WIRES

14 Clip off the wire's existing loop and remove the metal ball and coil; file the clipped end.

15 Use the round-nose pliers to form a new loop.

16 Using your fingers, gently reshape the ear wire body's curve into a flatter, wider arc (figure 3).

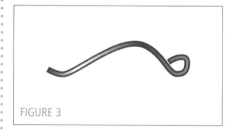

FIGURE 3

17 Attach the ear wire to the hoop's front loop. Adjust the tension in the ear wire's curve with the pliers so that the end secures properly into the back loop.

18 Repeat steps 14–17 to attach the other ear wire to the second earring.

MATERIALS

1 flat silver crystal briolette teardrop, 15 mm

2 round faceted aqua glass beads, 8 mm

2 smoky quartz faceted barrel beads, 11 mm

6 smooth apatite chips, 6 mm

2 clear glass beads, 3–4 mm

6 inches (15.2 cm) of 18-gauge uncoated brass wire

18 inches (45.7 cm) of 26-gauge uncoated brass wire

14 inches (35.6 cm) of 22-gauge uncoated brass wire

6 pieces of 22-gauge uncoated brass wire, each 3 inches (7.6 cm) long

2 pieces of uncoated brass cable chain, each 6 inches (15.2 cm) long

2 pieces of 22-gauge uncoated brass wire, each 2½ inches (6.4 cm) long

TOOLS

Round-nose pliers

Flat-nose pliers

Flush wire cutters

Diamond file

Round mandrel, ½ inch (1.3 cm) in diameter

Ball-peen hammer and steel block

Oxidizing solution for brass and copper

DIMENSIONS

Length, 18⅜ inches (46.7 cm)

Designed by DIANE MABREY

Smoky quartz, glass, and crystal gleam against oxidized brass in this modern look.

Quartz Crystal Necklace

Quartz Crystal Necklace

INSTRUCTIONS

Note: File all cut wire ends with the diamond file. Be sure to tuck the ends in so they won't scratch.

HORSESHOE ELEMENT

1 Use the wire cutters to cut a piece of the 18-gauge brass wire 2½ inches (6.4 cm) long. Form the wire into a horseshoe-shaped link over the mandrel.

2 Form a loop at each end with the round-nose pliers, then hammer them flat on the steel block. Also hammer the horseshoe shape.

3 Wrap the 26-gauge wire tightly and smoothly around the horseshoe shape. Use the wire cutters to trim any excess wire. Tuck the ends under one of the wraps with the flat-nose pliers.

4 Insert the 14-inch (35.6 cm) piece of 22-gauge wire into the crystal briolette. Shape the wire into a wrapped-loop cap at the narrow end. Set it aside.

ELEMENTS INTO STRANDS

5 Make a wrapped loop at one end of each of the six 3-inch (7.6 cm) pieces of 22-gauge wire. Connect the bead elements as follows:

Put an aqua glass bead onto one of the wrapped loops. Attach one end to one of the 6-inch (15.2 cm) pieces of chain with another wrapped loop.

Connect a quartz barrel bead to one of the free loops on a wrapped aqua bead loop.

Put three apatite chips onto one of the wires. Connect the group to the quartz barrel bead with a wrapped loop.

6 Using the remaining three 3-inch (7.6 cm) pieces of 22-gauge wire, repeat step 5 to connect:

- The other section of chain to the remaining aqua bead
- The barrel bead to the aqua bead
- The three remaining apatite chips to the quartz bead

FINAL CONNECTIONS

7 Open one of the loops on the Horseshoe Element with the flat-nose pliers. Slip the crystal briolette wrapped loop onto it. Add the strand you made in step 5, then close the loop.

8 Open the other loop in the Horseshoe Element. Add the strand you made in step 6, then close the loop.

9 Use the 2½-inch (6.4 cm) pieces of the 22-gauge brass wire to make the double wrapped loops that link the two clear glass beads to the free ends of the chain sections.

10 Cut a 2-inch (5.1 cm) piece of the remaining 18-gauge wire for the hook. Use the tip of the round-nose pliers to form a small loop. Reposition the pliers ½ inch (1.3 cm) away from it. Using a larger section of the pliers' jaws, bend the wire into a hook.

11 For the clasp's eye, trim the remainder of the 18-gauge wire into a 1-inch (2.5 cm) length. Form a small loop at one end. Use the pliers to turn the wire in the opposite direction of the small loop, making a larger loop at the other end. Hammer the two clasp pieces flat on the steel block.

12 Use the tips of the flat-nose pliers to open up the smaller loops on the clasp parts enough to connect them to the clear glass bead-wrapped loops at each end of the chain sections (figure 1). Close up the loops.

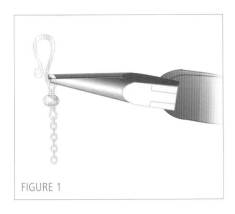

FIGURE 1

13 Dip the necklace into the oxidizing solution until you have obtained the desired degree of patina. Rinse the piece with water. Wipe it dry with a clean, soft cloth.

MATERIALS

10 pale pink crystal rondelles, 8 mm

40 inches (1.2 m) of 22-gauge non-tarnish silver wire

1 silver toggle clasp set

TOOLS

Round-nose pliers

Flat-nose pliers

Needle-nose pliers

Flush wire cutters

DIMENSIONS

Length, 8 inches (20.3 cm)

Designed by **JENNIFER FREITAS**

Delicate rose-colored crystals sparkle in this simple and classic silver design.

Rosaline Crystal Bracelet

INSTRUCTIONS

I Straighten the wire with your hands, then use flush wire cutters to cut ten 4-inch (10.2 cm) pieces from it.

2 Grasp one of the 4-inch (10.2 cm) pieces of wire 1½ inches (3.8 cm) from one end with the round-nose pliers. Turn the pliers full circle to create a small loop that measures 3–4 mm across (figure 1).

FIGURE 1

3 Holding the longer wire vertically, with its loop at the top, like a head pin, use flat-nose pliers to straighten out any kinks in it (figure 2).

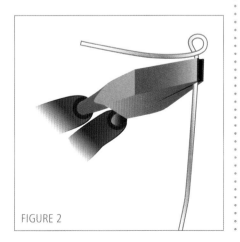

FIGURE 2

4 Hold the wire by its loop with flat-nose pliers. Grasp the end of the short tail with round-nose pliers and wrap it around the base of the loop three times. Closely cut any excess wire after you finish wrapping.

5 Use the needle-nose pliers to crimp the loop's wrapped base so there are no sharp edges sticking out. The remaining tail should measure 2½ inches (6.4 cm) long.

6 Slide a rondelle onto the tail. Bend the tail wire, ⁵⁄₁₆ inch (8 mm) from the bead, at a 90° angle.

7 Now wrap the newly bent wire around one jaw of your round-nose pliers to create another small wrapped loop, as you did at the other end. As you wrap, bring the wire as close to the crystal as possible; don't leave any space between the final wrap and the bead. Trim the wire as before and crimp the loop's base with the needle-nose pliers.

8 Create half a loop, 1½ inches (3.8 cm) from one end of the wire, from another 4-inch wire. Hook this half-loop into a loop on one end of the wrapped bead you just made. Use the needle-nose pliers to finish turning the loop.

9 Holding this new loop with the flat-nose pliers, wrap the short tail around the base of the wire three or four times with the round-nose pliers, in the same way as you did for the other loops you have made so far. Add a rondelle, then finish the wire with another wrapped loop.

IO Continue to connect the beads with wrapped loops until you have all used all but two of your rondelles.

II With one of the two remaining wire pieces, create a loop, 1½ inches (3.8 cm) from one end, with your round-nose pliers. Straighten the wire with the flat-nose pliers, as before. Make a half-loop and slide one half of the toggle clasp set into it. Close the loop and finish the wrapping and crimping, as before.

I2 Add the other half of the clasp in the same way: slide a rondelle onto the wire, then create a half-loop. Hook the half-loop onto one end of your string of linked rondelles, then close the loop, wrap the wire around the loop's base, and crimp the wrapping.

Designed by **JESSICA BARST**

Brown Iris Earrings

The sheen on this kind of fire-polished bead gives it a gleaming, eyelike iris. The natural burnish of brass wire matches perfectly.

MATERIALS

16 brown fire-polished faceted round Czech glass beads, 4 mm

2 pieces of dead-soft, round, non-tarnish brass wire, 14 gauge, each 3 inches (7.6 cm) long

2 pieces of dead-soft, round, non-tarnish brass wire, 24 gauge, each 16 inches (40.6 cm) long

1 pair of brass ear wires

TOOLS

Round-nose pliers

2 pairs of flat-nose pliers

Flush wire cutters

Sandpaper, 120 grit

Marker or dowel, ½ inch (1.3 cm) in diameter

Needle file

Jeweler's hammer and bench block

DIMENSIONS

Length, 1½ inches (3.8 cm)

INSTRUCTIONS

FRAMES

1 Smooth the burrs off the ends of the 14-gauge wires by rubbing them in circles on the sandpaper set on a hard, flat surface. Be sure to rotate and change the angle regularly to make a uniformly rounded end, instead of creating a beveled edge.

2 Use the round-nose pliers to make a loop in the end of the wire that you just smoothed. Grip the wire as close to the end as possible and turn it until it almost meets itself again (figure 1).

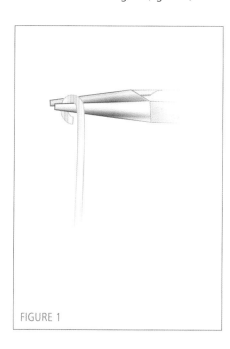

FIGURE 1

3 Use the marker or a dowel to form an S curve. Bend the wire around it in the direction opposite the smaller loop you just made, until the tail overlaps the rest of the piece.

4 Use the flush wire cutters to trim the excess wire, cutting at the point just before where the wire touches (figure 2).

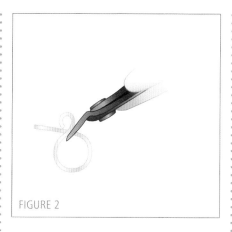

FIGURE 2

5 Bend this cut end out slightly (pulling it toward you if you are looking at the S piece straight on), and file the end smooth with the needle file. It's okay to have a lightly beveled edge this time, so that the end can meet the curve at an angle. Bend the smoothed end back into place to complete your first piece.

6 Repeat steps 2–6 for the second piece of wire. It's best to make sure your shapes match before moving on to the next step.

7 Hammer one S piece flat on the bench block, holding the other side of it steady with your thumb. Try to keep the thickness even all over. Turn the piece over and hammer the other side a few times, just to keep the piece flat, so it doesn't curve upward. Use the flat-nose pliers to bend the ends into place if the hammering has caused them to stretch or pull away. If necessary, use the file or sandpaper to smooth away any unwanted hammer or plier marks, or to create a nice brushed texture. Repeat for the second piece.

WRAPPING

8 Use the round-nose pliers to create a small loop ½ inch (1.3 cm) from the end of one of the 24-gauge wires.

9 Slip the small loop onto the open end of the bottom of the S shape, ⅛ inch (3 mm) from the opening. The shorter tail of wire should be on the side toward the top of the hoop. Pull the wire tight so the loop sits snugly against the hammered frame.

10 Wrap the short end of the wire around the frame three or four times, pulling it tight with each turn. Orient the frame as shown in figure 3. Use the flat-nose pliers to compress the wire wraps against the piece if necessary. Trim off the excess short tail with the flush wire cutters.

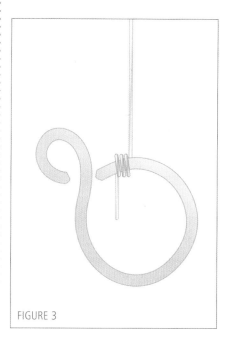

FIGURE 3

Brown Iris Earrings

11 Making sure the long tail of wire is pointing up and away from the hoop, add a 4-mm bead onto it. Loop the wire back around the frame again.

12 After each bead, wrap the wire around the frame two full times before adding another one, to keep the beads from twisting around on the frame. Continue adding beads and wrapping the wire until you have eight on the hoop. Make small adjustments to the beads' placement if you like.

13 Secure the end by wrapping the tail of the wire around the frame three or four times, just as you did at the start. Pull the tail back behind the last bead and wrap the wire around the frame once between the seventh and eighth beads.

14 Use the flush wire cutters to trim the tail of the wire on the back of the work so the cut end won't show.

FINISHING

15 Open one of the ear wires with the flat-nose pliers. Slide it through the top loop of the S shape. Use the pliers to squeeze the ear hook closed.

16 Repeat steps 9–15 for the other earring. This one must be a mirror image of the first earring, so check the frame's orientation before you start wrapping the wire around it.

Pearl Bracelet

You'll enjoy making silver wire swoop and scroll in this ladylike pearl-embellished bracelet.

Designed by COLETTE KIMON

MATERIALS

- 2 seamless sterling silver beads, 2.5 mm
- 8 round pearls, 6 mm
- 2 sterling silver fancy tube beads, 8 mm
- 2 pieces of soft sterling silver wire, 20 gauge, each 6½ inches (16.5 cm) long*
- 2 pieces of soft sterling silver wire, 28 gauge, each 4 inches (10.2 cm) long
- 3 pieces of soft sterling silver wire, 28 gauge, each 6 inches (15.2 cm) long
- 6 pieces of soft sterling silver wire, 22 gauge, each 4 inches (10.2 cm) long
- 4 inches (10.2 cm) of large-link chain or extender chain
- 10 sterling silver jump rings, 3 mm
- 1 sterling silver head pin, 22 gauge
- 1 oval sterling silver lobster clasp, 3.5 mm, with jump ring

* I balled the ends of the 20-gauge wire myself with a torch, but you can purchase fancy ball or bali-style head pins instead. They're available at most jewelry websites and supply stores. Be aware, though, that only one end will have a ball end.

TOOLS

Round-nose pliers

Flush wire cutters

2 pairs of flat-nose pliers

DIMENSIONS

Length, 8⁹⁄₁₆ inches (21.7 cm)

INSTRUCTIONS

FOCAL ELEMENT

1 Position the widest part of the round-nose pliers in the middle of one of the 6½-inch (16.5 cm) 20-gauge wires. Cross the wires around one jaw of the pliers to form a loop (figure 1). This will be the center loop in one of the focal units.

FIGURE 2

FIGURE 3

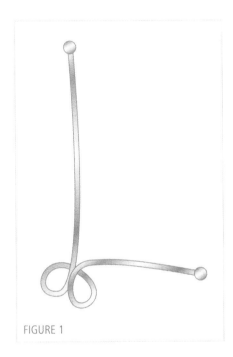

FIGURE 1

2 Remove the pliers' jaw from the first loop. Grasp a section of wire to the immediate right of it, ½ inch (1.3 cm) from the end of the pliers' jaw. Bring the wire's end around the jaw, being sure to loop the wire in, toward the first (center) loop (figure 2). Do the same with the wire to the left of the main loop.

3 Starting on the right side, grasp the tip of the right-hand tail with the round-nose pliers. Curve it until the tip is in the right-hand loop. Reposition the pliers as needed to continue curving the wire until its tip extends 1 inch (2.5 cm) beyond this new loop (figure 3). Do the same with the left-hand tail.

4 Using the tip of the round-nose pliers, form a small loop at the end of the right-hand tail. Reposition the round-nose pliers into the small loop you just made so you can curve the wire out (to the right) and down. Tuck the end neatly into the last loop you made. Repeat this step for the left tail. This is one half of the scrolled focal unit.

5 Repeat steps 1–4 for the other side of the unit.

6 Use a 4-inch (10.2 cm) piece of 28-gauge wire to attach one of the silver beads to the space between the two scrolled focal units, as shown in figure 4. Trim any excess wire. When you hold it with the center loop pointing down, it looks like a figure with wings.

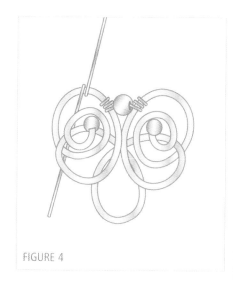

FIGURE 4

7 Repeat step 7 to add a silver bead to the second unit in the same way.

FOCAL UNIT
8 Wrap a 6-inch (15.2 cm) piece of the 28-gauge wire once around the "shoulder" of the one of the "wings." Bring the wire up to the front of the work. Position the second unit upside down, shoulders touching. Wrap the top of the wing wire (figure 5). Cut the excess and crimp the end with the pliers.

FIGURE 5

9 Repeat step 8 to join the other two wings in the same way.

10 Wrap one end of the remaining 6-inch (15.2 cm) piece of 28-gauge wire to the top of the center loop, as shown in figure 6. Slide a pearl onto the wire, centering it between the two joined

halves of the focal unit. Finish wrapping the wire on the other side. Cut the wire and tuck in the end. Crimp the ends with the pliers if necessary.

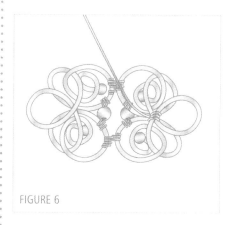

FIGURE 6

BRACELET ELEMENTS
11 From a 4-inch (10.2 cm) piece of 22-gauge wire, make a wrapped-pearl loop. Catch one loop end in one of the focal unit's center loops. Use another wire and pearl to do the same on the other center loop.

12 Use a pair of jump rings to attach each tube bead to the free end of a pearl loop. Open the rings with the flat-nose pliers.

13 Make another pair of wrapped-pearl loops with the remaining 4-inch (10.2 cm) pieces of 22-gauge wire. Connect one end of each pearl loop to the free end of a tube bead with a pair of jump rings. Attach the section of extender chain to one of the free ends of a wrapped loop with a pair of jump rings.

ADD FINAL ELEMENTS

14 Make a final wrapped-pearl loop with the head pin, attaching it to the end of the chain.

15 Attach the lobster clasp to the last wrapped-pearl loop by its jump ring. Use a pair of jump rings to attach the free end of the chain to the free end of the wrapped-pearl loop.

Back view

MATERIALS

- 1 golden brown resin rhinestone bead, 14 mm
- 4 feet (1.2 m) of golden silver-plated wire, 20 gauge*

TOOLS

Flat-nose pliers with nylon-coated jaws

Ring mandrel

Flush wire cutters

* This is enough wire for any size ring, with some left over.

DIMENSIONS

Height, 1½ inches (3.8 cm)

Designed by SNOW FAWN WHITNEY

Resin Rhinestone Ring

Don't judge…get your bling the old-fashioned way by making this super simple finger-sparkler.

INSTRUCTIONS

1 Fold the wire in half and string the rhinestone bead into the bend in the middle. Cross the wires so the bead stays in place.

2 Wrap a small strip of paper or a string around your ring finger, then match it to a size on the ring mandrel. Place the bead and wire on the ring mandrel line that is one size bigger than the desired size.

Resin **Rhinestone Ring**

3 Use your fingers to wrap the wires around the mandrel twice, in opposite directions. You should have four wires across the back of the mandrel now. This is the ring's band. The tails should be standing up on either side of the bead.

4 Bring one of the tails around to the side of the ring and tightly wrap it around all four of the band's wires once (figure 1). Use the flat-nose pliers to finish pulling each wrap. Make the same wrap on the other side of the bead.

5 Wrap the remaining wire, in opposite directions, of both tails around the base of the bead. Stop when you have 1½ inches (3.8 cm) of tail left on each end.

6 Make several coils around the sides of the band with the last bit of each tail.

7 Pull the wire tightly to the inside of the band. Use the flush wire cutters to snip the wire very close to the band (figure 2). Use the flat-nose pliers to squeeze the wire end down flush to the band. Now slide the finished ring as far as possible down on the mandrel to tighten the wirework.

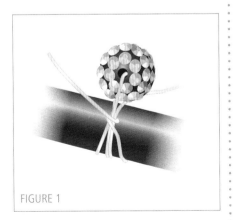

FIGURE 1

FIGURE 2

MATERIALS

1 flower-themed lamp work bead, 15 mm

3 faux creamy white pearls, 8 mm

2 pale mauve Czech fire-polished and faceted round glass beads, 8 mm

1 faux pale pink pearl, 10 mm

48 inches (1.2 m) of silver-plated non-tarnish wire, 18 gauge

TOOLS

Round-nose pliers (optional)

Tape measure

Felt-tip pen

Dowel (crochet hook, knitting needle) just large enough to make a bail that lets your chain pass through it

Flush wire cutters

DIMENSIONS

$1\frac{5}{16}$ x $1\frac{9}{16}$ inches (3.3 x 4 cm)

Designed by KANDYCE RAMPLING

Flowered Lamp Pendant

Dramatic swirls, Czech glass, and pearls encase one lovely-as-a-summer's-day lampwork focal bead in this stunning pendant.

Flowered Lamp Pendant

INSTRUCTIONS

1 Measure and mark the center point of the wire, then string the flower lamp work bead to the mark.

2 Holding the bead so that its hole is vertical, fold the bottom, or "wrapping," wire one and a half times around the bead. The wrapping wire will now be at the top of the bead with the "stem" wire (figure 1).

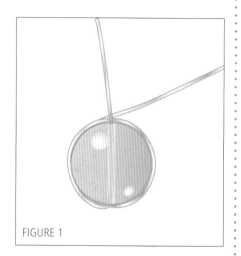

FIGURE 1

3 Carry the wrapping wire tightly around the stem wire two or three times so that it's snug to the top of the bead.

4 Bring the wrapping wire to the back side of the bead. Make a loop on that side to keep the bead stationary, so that it will always face the right way. This loop should be three-quarters the size of the bead (figure 2). Wrap the wrapping wire around the stem wire two or three times to make a shank.

FIGURE 2

5 String a white pearl onto the wrapping wire and slide it completely down.

6 Wrap the wire around the pearl two or three times, bringing it back to the top when you're done.

7 Wrap the wrapping wire two or three times around the wire that protrudes from the top of the glass bead so as to form a small shank (figure 3).

FIGURE 3

8 Add one of the Czech beads to the wrapping wire and wrap the bead as described in steps 6 and 7 (figure 4). Add the rest of the beads in this way and in this order: creamy white pearl, creamy white pearl, Czech bead, pink pearl. Be sure to add wraps around the stem wire each time to secure the beads' positions and strengthen your finished pendant.

FIGURE 4

9 When all the beads are strung and wrapped onto your pendant, you can make adjustments and tighten their positioning with the wrapping wire.

10 To make the chain loop (for a bail) at the top of the pendant, straighten the stem wire by pulling it and centering it at the back of your pendant.

11 Wrap the stem wire around a dowel, crochet hook, or knitting needle two or three times, ending with your wire at the bottom of the loop.

12 Secure the chain loop. Do neat wire wraps with the wrapping wire until it reaches the body of the pendant. Remove the dowel.

13 Using what's left of the wrapping and stem wires and, working from the back side, make five decorative loops that extend beyond the profile of the pendant. Twist the base of each loop to secure it.

14 If any beads aren't positioned quite as you'd like them to be or seem a little wobbly, secure them with any remaining wrapping wire.

15 Trim the tail and stem wires, leaving a 1-inch (2.5 cm) tail on each wire. Tuck the cut ends into the back of your pendant, or curl them with round-nose pliers into neat little spirals instead.

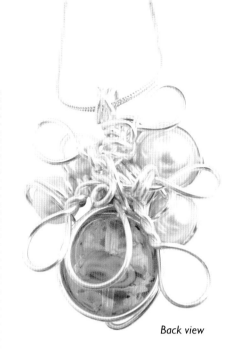

Back view

MATERIALS

2 dark purple faceted Lucite teardrop beads, 12 mm

2 tan Czech glass pyramid beads, 8 mm

2 striped orange teardrop glass beads, 12 mm

1 striped orange round glass bead, 12 mm

1⅜ inches (3.5 cm) of steel wire, 19 gauge

2 pieces of steel wire, 24 gauge, each 6 inches (15.2 cm) long

2 pieces of steel wire, 24 gauge, each 14 inches (35.6 cm) long

3 pieces of steel wire, 24 gauge, each 12 inches (30.5 cm) long

10 inches (25.4 cm) of steel wire, 24 gauge

1 vintage metal button or other shank-style charm, 10 mm

8 claw-style oxidized brass bead caps

4 prong-style oxidized brass bead caps

4 flat oxidized petal-style bead caps

4 filigree-style oxidized bead caps

1 filigree-style oxidized brass connector with 2 loops

TOOLS

Round-nose pliers

Cloth

Microcrystalline wax

Cotton swabs

Flush wire cutters

Jeweler's file

DIMENSIONS

Length, 8 inches (20.3 cm)

Designed by RICHELLE HAWKS

Rich metal texture plus chunky beads wrapped in steel give this bracelet a Goth-style air.

Lucite & Glass Bracelet

INSTRUCTIONS

1 Wipe each piece of wire with the cloth. Seal the wires with a light coat of the wax applied with a cotton swab. You may choose to file both ends of the wire after initially cutting it from the spool, but I find it more convenient and practical to file the working end of the wire only when its work is done in case the wire needs to be trimmed a bit.

HOOK CLASP

2 Make a closed loop in one end of the 1⅜-inch (3.5 cm) piece of steel wire.

3 Holding the wire by the loop, place the pliers a little less than halfway down the length of the wire. Make a sharp bend in the wire so the straight end is a tiny bit past the loop.

4 Using the pliers, make a slight bend at the wire's tip, pointing away from the loop.

5 Attach the vintage button to the loop. Leave the hook's loop open slightly for the upcoming first link attachment.

LINK I, LUCITE BEAD LINK

6 Make a loop in the middle of the 6-inch (15.2 cm) piece of wire. Wrap the base of the loop and leave the tail for the time being. This is the top loop. String onto the straight wire a claw-style bead cap, a prong-style bead cap, a Lucite teardrop bead (smaller end first), and a claw-style bead cap.

7 With the round-nose pliers, create a double loop with the wire from the bottom of the component (figure 1). Wrap

the base of the loop several times to close it. This is the bottom loop.

8 Neatly cover the base of the bead cap with wire. After several wraps, find a stopping place and cut any excess. File the end of the wire. Press the tip of the wire gently inward.

9 Return to the top loop and wrap the wire over the base of the bead cap. Cut and finish it as you did for the other end.

10 Attach this first beaded link to the hook's open loop (figure 2). Close the hook's loop, making certain the loop's ends are touching and there's no gap.

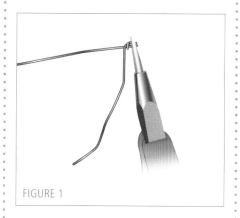

FIGURE 1

LINK 2, PYRAMID BEAD LINK

11 Create a loop a bit shy of halfway down one of the 14-inch (35.6 cm) pieces of wire. Wrap the wire under the loop's base to close it and leave the wire tail for now. This is the top loop.

12 String a pyramid bead onto the wire, small end first. Add a flat bead cap against the base of the bead. Make a loop with the pliers under the base of the bead cap, catching it in the loop of the teardrop bead link.

FIGURE 2

13 Holding the base of this loop with the pliers, wrap it several times to close the connection.

14 Make a cage-style wrap by bringing the wire up the side of the pyramid bead around the base of the top loop (figure 3), and back down around the base of the bead cap to secure it.

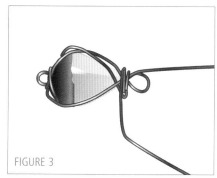

FIGURE 3

Lucite & Glass Bracelet

15 Bring the wire to the upper part of the component to continue this same wrapping action with the remaining wire tail, crisscrossing over the wire that's already wrapped around the bead. Keep your work tight and the wire straight and taut.

16 End the wrap near the bottom along the bead cap. Feed the ends under existing spaces in the wire to secure. Gently pull the wire end through and cut the excess if necessary. Finish the wrap with a tight, ornamental coil. The tip of the coil wire should point toward the bead cap (figure 4).

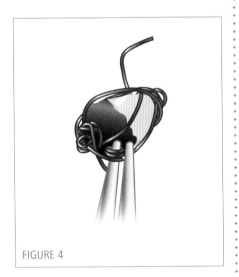

FIGURE 4

17 Use the end of the pliers' handle to push the coil flat against the bead cap.

LINK 3, TEARDROP BEAD LINK

18 Make a double loop in the middle of a 12-inch (30.5 cm) piece of wire. Wrap the loop to close it. Leave the wire tail for the time being. String onto the wire a claw-style bead cap, a filigree-style bead cap, a teardrop glass bead (larger end first), a prong-style bead cap, and a claw-style bead cap.

19 With the pliers, make a loop in the wire at the base of the component and attach it to the top loop of the pyramid bead link.

20 Close the loop by holding it at the base with the pliers and wrapping wire around it (figure 5). Cover the shaft (top) of the bead cap with plenty of wraps. Cut the wire if necessary and file it smooth. Gently press the tip of the wire in.

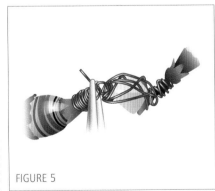

FIGURE 5

21 Complete the wire wrapping at the top of the component in the same way.

LINK 4, FOCAL LINK

22 Create a double loop in the middle of the 12-inch (30.5 cm) wire. String onto the wire a flat bead cap, a filigree bead cap, a round glass bead, a filigree bead cap, and a flat bead cap.

23 Create a loop with the round-nose pliers right next to the flat bead cap, catching it in the loop of the last link you made before you wrap it closed.

24 Keep wrapping the wire around the loop and over the top of the bead cap for a generous, ornamental wire cap.

25 Find a stopping place and clip the wire if necessary, filing the ends smooth. Press the tip of the wire in to finish the wrap.

26 Repeat this action with the other end of the wire under the loop and over the bead cap, clipping, filing, and pressing the wire to finish the wrapping. This link is the focal point of the design.

LINK 5, REVERSE TEARDROP BEAD LINK

27 Use the same materials and techniques as for Link 3 (teardrop bead), with the same looping, link connections, wrapping, and general techniques. Reverse the order of the bead caps, and string the smaller end of the teardrop bead first for this link.

LINK 6, REVERSE PYRAMID BEAD LINK

28 Use the instructions for Link 2 (pyramid bead), stringing the base of the pyramid bead first so that this link will be a mirror image of it.

LINK 7, REVERSE LUCITE BEAD LINK

29 Use the instructions for Link 1 (Lucite bead), stringing the large end of the Lucite bead first so that this link will be a mirror image of it.

CLASP WITH FAUX BEAD

30 Use the round-nose pliers to make a loop in the middle of the 10-inch (25.4 cm) wire. Catch this loop in the last bead link, then wrap the loop several times to close the connection.

31 Make the second loop, right up against the base of the first one, with the other wire end (figure 6).

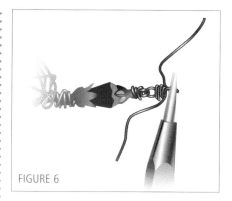

FIGURE 6

32 Catch the clasp connector in this loop, then close the connection with several wraps.

33 Alternate tightly wrapping each of the wire tails, one over the other, between the loop connections so they form a "faux bead" between the two loops. Clip the wire ends if necessary and file them.

34 Finish the wrap by pressing the ends gently inside the faux bead a bit and pressing down with the pliers to secure.

FINISH

35 Using a cloth, gently wipe any remaining carbon off the steel wire. Apply additional microcrystalline wax with a swab to the steel wire to seal it. Wipe any excess wax from the beads with an additional swab if necessary.

MATERIALS

- 2 olive green glass teardrops, 17 x 6 mm
- 4 faceted amethyst rondelles, 6 mm
- 2 pieces of copper wire, 20 gauge, each 2 inches (5.1 cm) long
- 2 copper balled head pins, 22 gauge, each 2 inches (5.1 cm) long
- 4 copper balled head pins, 24 gauge, each 1½ inches (3.8 cm) long
- 2 sections of textured copper 8 x 6 mm open-link chain, 3 links each

TOOLS

Round-nose pliers

2 pairs of chain-nose pliers

Small round mandrel

Flush wire cutters

Needle file

Ball-peen hammer and steel bench block

Liver of sulfur

Polishing cloth

DIMENSIONS

Length, 2 inches (5.1 cm)

Designed by SUSAN WALZ

The fresh color pairing in these teardrops takes its inspiration from a morning-bright vineyard.

Purple Olive Earrings

INSTRUCTIONS

EAR WIRES

1 Place one end of a 20-gauge wire ¼ inch (6 mm) from the tip of the pliers' jaws. Make a small loop on one end.

2 Hold the wire against the mandrel and bend it over the mandrel, away from the loop. Don't cut the wire yet.

3 Repeat steps 1 and 2 to make the second ear wire. Hold them together so you can see how much you need to trim the tails.

4 Use the round-nose pliers to make a small outward bend at the end of each ear wire.

5 Use the file to smooth the ear wires' cut ends.

6 Use the ball-peen hammer and steel bench block to lightly hammer and strengthen both ear wires.

WRAPPED BEAD LOOPS

7 String one teardrop bead onto a 22-gauge head pin.

8 Use the tip of the round-nose pliers to make a right-angle bend in the wire at the top of the teardrop.

9 Place the round-nose pliers at the bend and make a simple loop that will be large enough to fit through a link in the chunky textured chain (figure 1).

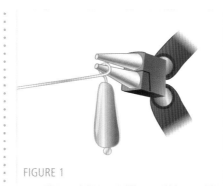

FIGURE 1

10 Use the chain-nose pliers to hold the loop. Use the second pair of chain-nose pliers to wrap the tail of the copper wire around the neck of the loop two or three times.

11 Use the cutters to snip the tail close to the wire wrapping. Use the chain-nose pliers to pinch the cut end into the wrapping.

12 String an amethyst rondelle onto one of the 24-gauge head pins. Follow steps 8–11 to wrap the rondelle.

13 Repeat steps 7–11 for all the remaining beads.

FINISHING

14 Use liver of sulfur to oxidize the ear wires, wrapped beads, and chain to the desired patina finish.

15 Use the polishing cloth to shine the metal. (You can tumble them for a higher polish than you can get with hand polishing.)

16 Use two pairs of chain-nose pliers to open an end link of the chunky textured copper chain. Attach one of the olive green teardrops, then close the link.

17 Use the chain-nose pliers to open the middle chain link. Attach one amethyst rondelle. Close the link using chain-nose pliers.

18 Use chain-nose pliers to open the other end link of the chain so you can slip an amethyst rondelle and an ear wire onto it. Close the link with the chain-nose pliers.

19 Repeat steps 16–18 for the second earring.

MATERIALS

13 pink ceramic beads, 6 mm

7 antique brass connector beads, 10 mm

15 antique brass filigree bead caps, 7 mm

4 antique brass head pins

7 antique brass eye pins

13 antique brass jump rings, 5 mm

1 antique brass jump ring, 7 mm

1 antique brass jump ring, 8 mm

42 inches (1.1 m) of antique brass chain*

* Some length will be lost due to cutting.

TOOLS

Round-nose pliers

2 pairs of flat-nose pliers

2 pairs of chain-nose pliers

Flush wire cutters

Tape measure

DIMENSIONS

Circumference, 30½ inches (77.5 cm)

Note: To create the matched dangle pairs, identify each with a number, 1 to 7, from left to right. The shortest pair would be 1 and 7, the next longer pair 2 and 6, and the longest dangle pair 3 and 5.

Designed by **NATHALIE MORNU**

Ceramic and metal marry in a swingy, superlength necklace made of brass chain and subtle bead choices.

Little Lanterns Necklace

INSTRUCTIONS

DANGLES #1 AND #7

1 String a pink bead onto a head pin and make a simple loop with round-nose pliers. Trim off any extra wire. Repeat, then set both elements aside.

2 Cut ½ inch (1.3 cm) of chain. Count the number of links in it and cut a second piece of chain that has the same quantity of links.

3 Use a 5-mm jump ring to attach one of the elements to one end of a piece of chain. Repeat to finish the second dangle. Set them aside.

DANGLES #2 AND #6

4 You'll work from the top down. String a bead cap and a pink bead onto an eye pin, then make a simple loop and trim off the extra wire. Use a 5-mm jump ring to attach the simple loop to one side of a metal bead.

5 Cut ½ inch (1.3 cm) of chain. Attach it to the other side of the metal bead using a 5-mm jump ring.

6 Dangle #2 is now finished. Make a second, identical dangle.

DANGLES #3 AND #5

7 Work from the top down. Cut ½ inch (1.3 cm) of chain and attach an eye pin to one end. On this eye pin, slide a bead cap and a pink bead, and close it with a simple loop (this creates a simple loop link). To this end, attach another simple loop link that also has a bead cap and a pink bead on it. To this second simple loop link, attach a metal bead. Set this aside for a moment. Slide a bead cap, a pink bead, and another bead cap onto a head pin and close it with a wrapped loop, catching the other side of the metal bead in the loop before closing it. This is dangle #3.

8 Make a second element identical to dangle #3.

CENTRAL DANGLE

9 You again work from the top down. Connect two metal beads to each other using the 7-mm jump ring, then set these aside momentarily. Using an eye pin, make a simple loop link with a bead cap and a pink bead on it. Attach the pair of metal beads to one side of the simple loop link, and attach another metal bead to the other side of the simple loop link.

Little Lanterns Necklace

10 Cut three pieces of chain, each 2 inches (5 cm) long. Use a 5-mm jump ring to attach them all to the bottom-most metal bead.

ATTACH THE DANGLES

11 Cut a piece of chain 18 inches (45.7 cm) long. Fold it in half to find the center link. Attach the top of the central dangle to this link, using the 8-mm jump ring.

12 Count three links to the left of the central dangle and attach the top of dangle #3 to this link, using a 5-mm jump ring. Count three links to the right of the central dangle and attach the top of dangle #5 to this link, again using a 5-mm jump ring.

13 Count three links to the left of dangle #3 and attach the top of dangle #2 to this link, using a 5-mm jump ring. Use another 5-mm jump ring to attach dangle #6 in the third link to the right of dangle #5.

14 Count four links to the left of dangle #2 and attach the top of dangle #1 to this link, once again using a 5-mm jump ring. Hang dangle #7 in the fourth link to the right of dangle #6, once again using a 5-mm jump ring.

FINISH THE CHAIN

15 Using the two remaining eye pins, make two simple loop links, each with a bead cap, a pink bead, and a bead cap on them.

16 Cut a piece of chain 11¾ inches (30 cm) long. Using one of the simple loop links, attach one end of it to one end of the chain that's 18 inches (45.7 cm) long. Attach the free end of the short chain to the free end of the long chain in the same manner.

Dancing Amethyst Earrings

These tiny blue-and-purple gems, finely wrapped, will have a party on your earlobes.

Designed by ELISABETH ALLERTON

MATERIALS

10 iolite rondelles, 3 mm

2 ice-blue quartz briolettes, 8 mm

4 moonstone rondelles, 4 mm

4 pink amethyst rondelles, 4 mm

4 crystal quartz rondelles, 3 mm

4 deep purple amethyst rondelles, 3 mm

2 pieces of sterling silver wire, 20 gauge, each 4 inches (10.2 cm) long

2 pieces of sterling silver wire, 28 gauge, each 3 inches (7.6 cm) long

2 pieces of sterling silver wire, 28 gauge, each 12 inches (30.5 cm) long

24 sterling silver knobby head pins, 28 gauge, each 3 inches (7.6 cm) long

TOOLS

Chain-nose pliers

Round-nose pliers

Mandrel

Flush wire cutters

Needle file

Liver of sulfur solution

Steel wool, grade 0000

Soft toothbrush (optional)

DIMENSIONS

Length, 1⁷⁄₁₆ inches (3.7 cm)

Dancing Amethyst Earrings

INSTRUCTIONS

1 Form one end of the 20-gauge wire over the mandrel into a circle that measures ¼ inch (6 mm) in diameter. Allow enough extra tail at this end so you can wrap the longer end twice around it. Keep the tail wire straight. Use the flush wire cutters to trim the tail wire 1½ inches (3.8 cm) from the wrap. This is the frame.

2 Use the chain-nose pliers to curve this straight tail wire three-quarters of the way around the mandrel. At its widest point, this circle will measure ⅜ inch (1 cm). This is the ear hook.

3 Bend the end of the ear hook wire slightly, then clip it 2 mm away from the bend (figure 1). File the tip, if desired, so it isn't as sharp.

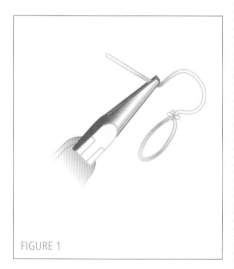

FIGURE 1

4 Wrap one of the 3-inch (8 cm) pieces of 28-gauge wire three or four times around the frame you made in step 1. Add one of the iolite rondelles, then wrap the remaining wire the same number of times on the other side of the

frame. Position the rondelle so that the drill hole is horizontal (figure 2). Trim the excess wire.

FIGURE 2

5 Insert the first 2 inches (5.1 cm) of a 12-inch (30.5 cm) piece of the 28-gauge wire through the briolette. Pinch the ends so they cross over each other directly above the tip of the briolette.

6 Wrap the longer end of the wire around the short end, again and again, until you have wrapped a shank that is ½ inch (1.3 cm) long.

7 Curve the wrapped shank over one jaw of the round-nose pliers so it forms a bail above the briolette (figure 3). Hook the bail onto the frame.

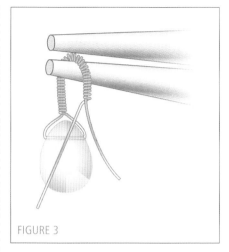

FIGURE 3

8 Wrap first the shorter end of the wire, then the remainder of the longer end, into a wire cap at the top of the briolette. Be sure to end your wrapping so that you can pull the last of the wire taut and cut it flush to the wrapping.

9 Divide the remaining 24 rondelles into four groups. Each group should contain:

- 2 iolites
- 1 moonstone
- 1 pink amethyst
- 1 crystal quartz
- 1 deep purple amethyst

I3 Finish the other earring in the same way, wrapping and adding wrapped bead loops to the frame.

I4 Oxidize the piece using liver of sulfur. When the desired degree of darkening has been reached, remove the earrings from the solution and rinse them thoroughly. Polish the earrings with the steel wool. If steel wool gets stuck in the crevices, use the toothbrush to get it out.

I0 Slide an iolite rondelle onto a head pin. Make a wrapped bead loop above the rondelle using round-nose pliers. Slide the loop onto the frame and to one side of the briolette. Wrap the end of the head pin a few times below the loop (figure 4). Cut off any excess head pin wire with the wire cutters, and tuck in the end.

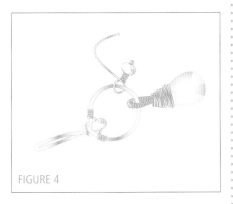

FIGURE 4

II Make five more wrapped rondelles. Add them to the frame, alongside the iolite you already added, in the order given in step 9. Start and end the group with an iolite rondelle.

I2 Repeat steps 10 and 11 on the other side of the briolette. There should be six wrapped bead loops on each side.

Quartz
Earrings

Rim a pair of stunning blue gemstones with fancy pearl dangles in this lavish design.

Designed by CLEOPATRA KERCKHOF

MATERIALS

- 12 white freshwater rice pearls, each $5/16$ inch (8 mm) long

- 2 blue quartz teardrop briolettes, 12 x 8 mm

- 2 pieces of dead-soft sterling silver wire, 26 gauge, each 24 inches (61 cm) long

- 2 pieces of dead-soft sterling silver wire, 26 gauge, each 6 inches (15.2 cm) long

- 12 sterling silver balled head pins, 28 gauge, each 1 inch (2.5 cm) long

- 2 sterling silver teardrop frames, 16 x 12 mm*

- 2 sterling silver closed jump rings, 4 mm

- 1 pair of sterling silver ear studs with 4-mm balls and open connector rings

* The teardrop opening in the frame should be a bit larger than the size of the briolette to allow for the wire wraps.

TOOLS

Round-nose pliers

2 pairs of flat-nose pliers

Chain-nose pliers

Flush wire cutters

Marker

Liver of sulfur

Steel wool, grade 0000

DIMENSIONS

Length, 1⅜ inches (3.5 cm)

INSTRUCTIONS

1 Use the round-nose pliers to form 12 wrapped bead loop dangles from the freshwater pearls and the sterling silver balled head pins. Set the dangles aside. You will add them later as you wrap the teardrop frames. It helps to grasp the loop with the flat-nose pliers as you wrap it closed. Trim the leftover wire with the cutters.

2 Use the marker to indicate the middle of the bottom of the teardrop frames. This will be your wrapping starting point.

3 Fold one length of the 24-inch (61 cm) sterling wire in half and slide it over the teardrop frame at the mark you made in step 2. Wrap the frame three times.

4 Thread the first dangle onto the wrapping wire and make a single wrap around the teardrop frame (figure 1). Be sure the dangle sits right at the bottom of the frame and that it can still wiggle.

FIGURE 1

5 Wrap the frame another three times, thread another dangle, and wrap the frame once. Wrap the frame three more times.

6 Add a third dangle with a single wrap, then wrap the frame three more times. At this point, make sure the wrapping is nice and close together and the dangles are positioned correctly.

Adjust if necessary.

7 Use the other half of the wrapping wire to add three dangles on the other half of the teardrop shape. Check the positions of the dangles and adjust them if necessary.

8 Continue to wrap both sides until there is just a small bare spot at the top of the teardrop frame.

9 Slip one of the closed rings onto one of the wrapping wire's tails and down to the top of the teardrop. Secure it there by wrapping it three times. Tuck that tail through the three wraps on what will be the back of the earring and pull it taut with the chain-nose pliers (figure 2). Wrap and tuck the other wire in the same way but in the opposite direction. If the wrapping is too tight to slide the tail through it, simply cut the tail and press it in between two of the wraps with the chain-nose pliers. Flatten all of the wraps gently with the chain-nose pliers.

FIGURE 2

Earrings

10 Center one of the briolettes on one of the 6-inch (15.2 cm) wires. Lay the bead on the wire across the wrapped teardrop frame.

11 Coil the wire twice around the teardrop frame and bring it back to the front (figure 3). Make sure the wire is nice and tight using the chain-nose pliers. The briolette should sit straight and not sag. Do the same wrap on the other side, and bring the wire to the front. Don't trim the wires yet.

FIGURE 3

12 Wrap the waiting wire tail around the horizontal wire that runs through the briolette in the space between the side of the briolette and the frame. Make sure the briolette is nicely centered by wrapping the wire an equal number of times on each side. Trim the wires and gently press them against the wraps with the very tip of the chain-nose pliers. You should be able to move the bead just a little bit.

13 Repeat steps 3–12 to make the other earring.

14 Use two pairs of pliers to open the ear stud's connector ring and attach it to the ring at the top of the teardrop frame. Add the stud to the other earring.

15 Apply the liver of sulfur solution to the wire parts of the earrings. Polish the silver with the steel wool.

Wire Gauge Chart

The standards for wire diameters differ in the United States and the United Kingdom. AWG is the acronym for American, or Brown & Sharpe, wire gauge sizes and their equivalent rounded metric measurements. SWG is the acronym for the British Standard, or Imperial, system used in the UK. This book lists wire using the American system. Refer to the chart below if you use SWG wire. (Only part of the full range of wire gauges is included here.)

AWG IN.	AWG MM	GAUGE	SWG IN.	SWG MM
0.204	5.18	4	0.232	5.89
0.182	4.62	5	0.212	5.38
0.162	4.12	6	0.192	4.88
0.144	3.66	7	0.176	4.47
0.129	3.28	8	0.160	4.06
0.114	2.90	9	0.144	3.66
0.102	2.59	10	0.128	3.25
0.091	2.31	11	0.116	2.95
0.081	2.06	12	0.104	2.64
0.072	1.83	13	0.092	2.34
0.064	1.63	14	0.080	2.03
0.057	1.45	15	0.072	1.83
0.051	1.30	16	0.064	1.63
0.045	1.14	17	0.056	1.42
0.040	1.02	18	0.048	1.22
0.036	0.914	19	0.040	1.02
0.032	0.813	20	0.036	0.914
0.029	0.737	21	0.032	0.813
0.025	0.635	22	0.028	0.711
0.023	0.584	23	0.024	0.610
0.020	0.508	24	0.022	0.559
0.018	0.457	25	0.020	0.508
0.016	0.406	26	0.018	0.457

About the Designers

Elisabeth Allerton
Walpole, Massachusetts
elisabethallerton@yahoo.com
www.elisabethallerton.etsy.com

Jerrie Anderson
Rolla, Missouri
Three Cheep Chicks
threecheepchicks@gmail.com
www.threecheepchicks.com
www.threecheepchicks.etsy.com

Jessica Barst
Fort Worth, Texas
Bespangled Jewelry
jess@bespangled.com
www.bespangled.com
www.bespangledjewelry.blogspot.com

Marie Castiglia
Rochester, New York
Designs By Missrie
designsbymissrie@gmail.com
www.missrie.etsy.com

Sharon Clancy
Sedona, Arizona
Sharon Clancy Designs
www.sharonclancydesigns.etsy.com

Barbra Davis
Asheville, North Carolina
Wired Women Designs
emama333@yahoo.com
www.wiredwomendesigns.com
www.etsy.com/shop/wiredwomendesigns

Brenda Davis
Asheville, North Carolina
Wire_lover@yahoo.com
www.wiredwomendesigns.com
www.etsy.com/shop/wiredwomendesigns

Jennifer Freitas
New Bedford, Massachusetts
Isaac & Rebekah
isaac.and.rebekah@hotmail.com
www.facebook.com/isaacandrebekah
www.jennoveev.blogspot.com

Colleen Gilgenbach
Asheville, North Carolina
gilgenbachdesigns@gmail.com

Inna Gor
Toronto, Ontario, Canada
www.ingojewelry.com
www.ingodesign.etsy.com

Richelle Hawks
Little Falls, New York
Shipwreck Dandy
shipwreckdandy@yahoo.com
www.etsy.com/shop/shipwreckdandy
www.shipwreckdandy.blogspot.com

Cleopatra Kerckhof
Hemiksem, Belgium
cleopatra.kerckhof@pandora.be
www.cleopatrakerckhof.etsy.com
www.bead-you-to-it.com

Colette Kimon
Morgantown, West Virginia
www.colettecollection.com

Coco Kulkarni
Toronto, Ontario, Canada
Coco's Jewelry
cocokulkarni@gmail.com
www.cocosjewelry.etsy.com

Diane Mabrey
Diane Mabrey Designs
diane_mabrey@sbcglobal.net
www.dianemabrey.com
www.dianedesign.etsy.com

Yuko Machida
Saitama, Japan
Yuko Jewelry
yuko@yukojewelry.com
www.yukojewelry.com

Nathalie Mornu
Asheville, North Carolina
www.larkcrafts.com/jewelry-beading

Kammy Pietraszek
Woodinville, Washington
Sugar Rococo
kammylnp@gmail.com
www.sugarrococo.etsy.com

Kandyce Rampling
Waterford, Ontario, Canada
waterfordcollectables@sympatico.ca

Bonnie Riconda
Bronx, New York
Calico Juno Designs
calicojunodesigns@msn.com
www.calicojunodesigns.com
www.etsy.com/shop/calicojunojewelry

Rebecca Sanchez
Long Beach, California
South Wind Design
southwinddesign@yahoo.com
www.southwinddesign.etsy.com
www.facebook.com/southwnd

Nancy Scott and Laura B. Scott
Panama City, Florida
Bees & Buttercups Jewelry
info@beesandbuttercups.com
www.beesandbuttercups.com
www.beesandbuttercups.etsy.com

Gordon Strickland
Chelsea, Alabama
carolvs40@hotmail.com
www.serendipitousstuff.com
ww.etsy.com/shop/carolvs40

Kendra Tornheim
Belmont, Massachusetts
Silver Owl Creations
silverowlcreations@gmail.com
www.silverowlcreations.com
www.etsy.com/shop/silverowlcreations

Susan Walz
Center Valley, Pennsylvania
DreamBelle Designs
dreambelledesigns@hotmail.com
www.dreambelledesign.etsy.com

Snow Fawn Whitney
Stetson, Maine
Twisting Bobbles on Facebook
snoiefrog@aol.com
www.etsy.com/shop/twistingbobbles

About the Author

Suzanne Tourtillott is an independent writer and mini-publisher who collaborates with designers and authors in the making of books on craft. She is lucky to live in Asheville, North Carolina, with her cat, Miette, and an ever-growing brood of grands.

Acknowledgments

This book would not be possible without the talented and hardworking artists who shared their lovely jewelry designs and secret wire techniques. To them, my huge and heartfelt thanks. I'd also like to thank Lark Jewelry & Beading team extraordinaire Nathalie, Ray, Hannah, Kathy, and Carol for faith, advice, and patience; the unflappable Jackie at Chevron Trading Post & Bead Company in Asheville, North Carolina; my own brilliantly creative team of Mary McG and Melissa G.S., who are nothing if not light on their feet; and finally, huge love to family and friends who always support in big ways and small.

Index

More Books for Bead & Wire Fun!

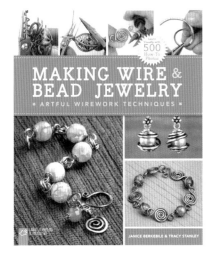

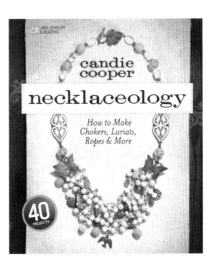

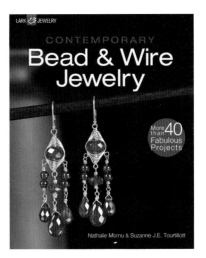

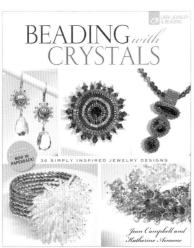

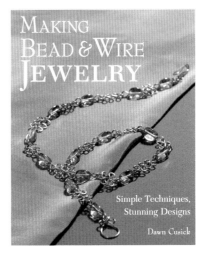

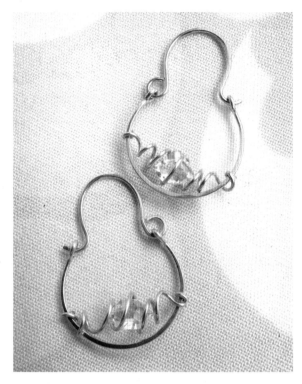